Gooseberry Patch

MEALS in MinuteS

Gooseberry Patch

An imprint of Globe Pequot
64 South Main Street
Essex, CT 06426

www.gooseberrypatch.com

1•800•854•6673

Do you have a tried & true recipe...

tip, craft or memory that you'd like to see featured in
a **Gooseberry Patch** cookbook? Visit our website at
www.gooseberrypatch.com, register and follow the
easy steps to submit your favorite family recipe.
Or send them to us at:

Gooseberry Patch
PO Box 812
Columbus, OH 43216-0812

Don't forget to include the number of servings your recipe makes,
plus your name, address, phone number and email address. If we
select your recipe, your name will appear right along with it...
and you'll receive a **FREE** copy of the book!

Contents

Dedication

To all of our **Gooseberry Patch**
family & friends who have inspired us
through countless family mealtimes,
get-togethers and celebrations...
you're simply the best.

Appreciation

For sending us your best-loved
recipes and your favorite kitchen
tips & tricks over the years...we
can't thank you enough!

Market Fresh & Fast

Fresh Pasta Salad

Mary Forsythe
Frontenac, KS

This picnic-perfect salad makes a great lunch too!

16-oz. pkg. rotini
8-oz. can tomato sauce
1 c. Italian salad dressing
1 T. fresh basil, chopped
1 T. fresh oregano, chopped
1 c. sliced mushrooms

5 roma tomatoes, chopped
1 cucumber, chopped
1 sweet onion, chopped
2-1/4 oz. can sliced olives,
  drained

Cook pasta according to package directions; drain. Rinse with cold water; pour into a serving bowl and set aside. Combine remaining ingredients; mix gently. Pour over pasta; toss to coat. Cover and refrigerate until serving. Makes 8 servings.

White Corn Casserole

Carol Hickman
Kingsport, TN

Sweet corn with a touch of honey...what could be better?

6 ears corn, husked
1/2 c. butter, melted
1/4 c. honey
1/2 c. all-purpose flour

2 eggs, separated
1/2 c. milk
1/4 t. salt
1/2 t. pepper

Slice corn from cobs; set aside. Mix butter and honey together; add flour and egg yolks. Blend until smooth; add milk. Stir in corn, salt and pepper; set aside. Whip egg whites until stiff peaks form; gently fold into corn mixture. Pour into a greased 1-1/2 quart casserole dish; bake, uncovered, at 350 degrees for 45 minutes. Serves 4 to 6.

Vegetable Pizza

Remona Putman
Rockwood, PA

Broccoli, cauliflower, sweet peppers...use your favorite fresh veggies!

2 8-oz. tubes refrigerated
   crescent rolls
8-oz. pkg. cream cheese,
   softened
2 T. dill weed
2 T. onion, chopped
1 t. seasoned salt

3/4 c. mayonnaise
3/4 c. mayonnaise-type
   salad dressing
1-1/2 c. assorted fresh
   vegetables, chopped
8-oz. pkg. shredded Cheddar
   cheese

Spread out rolls on a lightly greased baking sheet, pinching seams together; bake at 375 degrees for 5 minutes. Set aside. Blend cream cheese, dill weed, onion, seasoned salt, mayonnaise and salad dressing together; spread over rolls. Arrange vegetables evenly over the top; press lightly into cream cheese mixture. Sprinkle with cheese; cut into squares to serve. Serves 24.

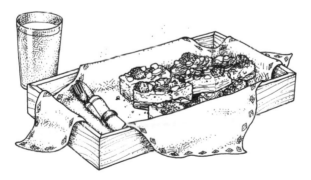

Make assembly part of pizza-making fun! Roll out
refrigerated biscuits to individual pizza-size crusts and
bake until golden. Pass them out to family members,
set out the sauce, veggies, seasonings and cheese
to top. Slice into quarters and dinner's done!

7th-Heaven Layered Salad

Faye LaRosa
McKeesport, PA

*All the goodness of a tossed salad...it's tastiest
when made a day ahead!*

8-oz. pkg. cream cheese,
  softened
1 c. mayonnaise
1 c. sour cream
1 t. dried basil
1/2 t. garlic powder
1/2 t. onion powder
1/2 head lettuce, torn
2 tomatoes, chopped

1 cucumber, sliced
3 carrots, peeled and sliced
10 to 12 green onions, finely
  chopped
8-oz. pkg. shredded sharp
  Cheddar cheese
1 lb. bacon, crisply cooked
  and crumbled

In a bowl, combine cream cheese, mayonnaise, sour cream and seasonings. Cover and set aside. In a 13"x9" glass baking pan, layer lettuce, tomatoes, cucumber, carrots and onions; spoon cream cheese mixture over the top. Sprinkle with Cheddar cheese and bacon. Cover and refrigerate until serving. Serves 12.

When frying bacon for this salad, reserve a few pieces. Slice
a homegrown tomato into fat slices and add lettuce for a
fresh BLT sandwich...tomorrow's lunch is ready!

Roasted Veggie Panini

Lynda McCormick
Burkburnett, TX

*One of my family's favorite sandwiches...it's especially good
in the summertime when veggies are abundant.*

2 zucchini, thickly sliced
1 yellow squash, thickly sliced
8 oz. pkg. portabella
  mushrooms
2 t. olive oil, divided
1 t. balsamic vinegar
1 sweet onion, sliced

1 loaf sourdough bread, sliced
1 red pepper, thickly sliced
1 green pepper, thickly sliced
1 yellow pepper, thickly sliced
1 c. spinach leaves
2 roma tomatoes, sliced
4 slices provolone cheese

Combine zucchini, squash and mushrooms in a large bowl; toss with
one teaspoon olive oil and vinegar. Grill or broil until tender; set aside.
Sauté onion in remaining olive oil in a skillet over medium heat until
caramelized; set aside. Spread tops and bottoms of bread slices with
desired amount of Olive Tapenade; layer peppers, spinach, tomatoes
and cheese evenly on half the bread slices. Top with veggies and
remaining bread slices; grill or broil lightly on both sides. Makes 4.

Olive Tapenade:

6-oz. jar pitted green olives,
  drained
1 shallot, chopped

1 t. lemon juice
1/8 t. pepper
1/2 c. olive oil

Pulse ingredients in a food processor until desired consistency is
achieved. Refrigerate any remaining mixture in an airtight container.
Makes about 1/2 cup.

Cauliflower Soup

Tina Wright
Atlanta, GA

A hearty and simple soup full of good-for-you veggies.

1 head cauliflower, cut into
    flowerets
5 c. chicken broth
1/4 c. celery, finely chopped
1/2 c. instant rice, uncooked

1 c. milk or half-and-half
1/4 c. all-purpose flour
salt and pepper to taste
Garnish: sliced green onions,
    chopped fresh parsley

In a large saucepan, combine cauliflower, broth, celery and rice; bring to a boil. Reduce heat and simmer 10 minutes, or until cauliflower is crisp-tender and rice is cooked. In a bowl, gradually whisk milk or half-and-half into flour until smooth; stir into soup. Bring to a boil, stirring constantly until thickened. Season to taste and garnish as desired. Makes 6 servings.

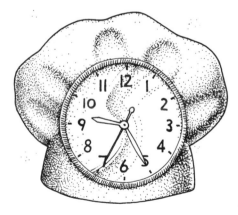

In my grandmother's house there was always chicken soup
And talk of the old country...
–Louis Simpson

Stir-Fried Sesame Vegetables
*Jill Ross
Columbus, OH*

This dish is a delicious and easy way to use the bounty from your garden. It's simple to substitute the veggies for whatever is in season!

1-1/2 c. vegetable broth	1 yellow onion, sliced
3/4 c. long-grain rice, uncooked	2 c. sliced mushrooms
1 T. margarine	2 t. fresh ginger, minced
2 T. peanut oil	1 t. garlic, minced
1/2 lb. asparagus, cut into 1-inch pieces	3 T. soy sauce
1 red pepper, cut into 1-inch pieces	1 T. sesame oil
	1 T. sesame seed, toasted

In a saucepan, combine broth, rice and margarine. Cover and bring to a boil over high heat. Reduce heat to low and simmer, covered, for 15 minutes. Meanwhile, heat peanut oil in a large skillet over medium high heat. Add vegetables, ginger and garlic; stir-fry for 4 to 5 minutes, or until crisp-tender. Stir in soy sauce and cook for 30 seconds. Remove from heat; stir in sesame oil and sesame seed. Serve over rice. Serves 4.

Melon balls, frozen berries and pineapple chunks make yummy fruit kabobs. Try 'em with ooey-gooey fondue...just melt chocolate chips with a little milk or cream and dip away!

Country-Time Green Beans

Sheri Fuchser
Goodlettsville, TN

The secret to perfect green beans every time? Don't snap off the ends of fresh green beans until they've been cooked and cooled.

1 lb. green beans
3/4 T. butter
3/4 T. all-purpose flour
3/4 t. sugar
1/3 c. chicken broth, warmed

3/4 t. cider vinegar
pepper to taste
3 slices bacon, crisply cooked
    and crumbled

Boil green beans in water, uncovered, for 2 minutes. Drain; plunge beans into cold water. Drain; cut off stems and ends. Set aside. In a skillet over medium heat, melt butter; whisk in flour until smooth. In a small bowl, combine sugar and broth; add to flour mixture. Bring to a boil; stir for one minute. Reduce heat; mix in vinegar without boiling. Season with pepper; add beans and bacon. Heat through. Serves 6.

Country-Time Green Beans are delicious alongside
Bacon-Wrapped Chicken (on page 143). Crispy
bacon in both makes them extra yummy!

Zucchini-Tomato Casserole *Sandy Benham*
Sanborn, NY

This is one of my favorite casseroles since it helps to use up the zillions of zucchini in my garden!

1 c. green onions, sliced	1/2 t. dried basil
5 c. zucchini, cubed	1/2 t. dried oregano
1 clove garlic, minced	1/2 t. paprika
2 T. garlic salt	1-1/2 c. cooked rice
2 tomatoes, chopped	2 c. shredded Cheddar cheese

In a skillet over medium heat, sauté onions, zucchini and garlic until tender; set aside. Combine remaining ingredients; add onion mixture. Spread into a greased 1-1/2 quart casserole dish. Bake, uncovered, at 350 degrees until heated through, about 25 minutes. Serves 4.

Cauliflower Salad

Barb Brosseau
Tinley Park, IL

Cool and creamy!

1 head lettuce, torn	1/2 c. onion, finely chopped
1 to 2 heads cauliflower, chopped	2 c. mayonnaise-type salad dressing
1 lb. bacon, crisply cooked and crumbled	1/4 c. grated Parmesan cheese
	1/4 c. sugar

In a large bowl, toss lettuce, cauliflower, bacon and onion; set aside. Combine remaining ingredients; fold into lettuce mixture. Cover and refrigerate until serving. Makes 8 servings.

Easy Enchilada Casserole

Heather Bass
Moore, OK

Great with homemade salsa and lots of
crispy chips on the side...olé!

15-oz. bag tortilla chips, divided
2 c. shredded Cheddar cheese,
   divided
10-3/4 oz. can cream of
   chicken soup

10-oz. can enchilada sauce
16-oz. can green chile sauce

Arrange a layer of chips over the bottom of a greased 13"x9" baking
pan; sprinkle one cup Cheddar cheese on top. In a bowl, combine soup,
enchilada sauce and green chile sauce; spoon half over the cheese
layer. Add another layer of chips; top with remaining soup mixture.
Sprinkle with remaining cheese. Bake, uncovered, at 400 degrees for
30 minutes. Serves 6.

Leftover chicken? Shred and toss it in this zesty
casserole...serve up some Spanish rice on the side!

Mesa Corn Pie

Diane Visser-Johnston
Van Nuys, CA

A warm dish that has become tradition in our home.

14-3/4 oz. can creamed corn
1/4 c. milk
2 c. corn muffin mix
1 c. shredded Cheddar cheese

4-1/2 oz. can diced green chiles
3.8-oz. can sliced black olives,
   drained
2 T. butter, sliced

Pour corn into a greased 9"x9" casserole dish; add milk and mix well. Stir in corn muffin mix, Cheddar cheese, chiles and olives; mix well. Dot top with butter; bake, uncovered, at 350 degrees for 35 minutes. Cool 10 minutes before serving. Serves 6 to 8.

Chile-Cheese 'Taters

Carrie Andrews
Topeka, KS

Cheesy with just the right amount of kick!

32-oz. pkg. frozen seasoned
   potato wedges
1/2 c. butter, sliced
1 onion, chopped
4-1/2 oz. can diced green chiles,
   drained

12-oz. pkg. shredded mozzarella
   and Cheddar cheese blend
10-3/4 oz. can cream of
   mushroom soup
1-1/2 c. sour cream

Arrange a layer of potato wedges in a greased 13"x9" baking pan; dot with butter. Combine remaining ingredients; spread over potato wedges. Bake, uncovered, at 350 degrees for 45 to 60 minutes. Serves 4 to 6.

Almost-Instant Pierogies

Kristie Rigo
Friedens, PA

They'll be almost instantly gone too!

3 lbs. potatoes, peeled, quartered
   and boiled
2 c. shredded Cheddar cheese
1 t. salt
1/2 t. pepper

1/2 c. margarine
4 c. onions, sliced
12-oz. pkg. jumbo shell pasta,
   cooked

In a large bowl, combine potatoes and cheese; mash until smooth. Stir in salt and pepper; set aside. Melt margarine in a skillet; add onions. Sauté 10 to 15 minutes; spread half the onions in a lightly greased 13"x9" baking pan. Stuff each shell with potato mixture; arrange over onions. Sprinkle with remaining onions. Bake, uncovered, at 350 degrees for 20 to 25 minutes. Makes 6 to 8 servings.

Combine leftover mashed potatoes with minced onion
and cheese to taste. Pat into a round casserole dish and
bake until golden. Tastes like twice-baked potatoes
in half the time!

Cheesy Spinach Pie

Janine Kuras
Warren, MI

Two cheeses combine for a delectable dish.

2 c. cottage cheese	3 eggs, beaten
2/3 c. crumbled feta cheese	1/4 c. butter, melted
10-oz. pkg. frozen chopped	2 T. all-purpose flour
spinach, thawed and drained	2 t. dried, minced onion

In a large bowl, combine all ingredients; mix well. Spread into a greased 1-1/2 quart casserole dish. Bake, uncovered, at 350 degrees until center is set, about 45 minutes. Makes 8 servings.

Veggie Cheese Casserole

Pat France-Kelly
Columbia, MD

Canned veggies make this casserole ready in a jiffy.

2 15-oz. cans mixed vegetables	1/2 c. butter, melted
1 c. onion, chopped	1 sleeve round buttery crackers,
1 c. celery, chopped	crushed
1 c. mayonnaise	
1 c. pasteurized process cheese	
spread, shredded	

In a bowl, mix vegetables, mayonnaise and cheese; spread in a lightly greased 13"x9" baking pan. Combine butter and crackers; sprinkle on top. Bake, uncovered, at 350 degrees for 30 to 40 minutes. Makes 12 servings.

Add frozen mixed veggies to scrambled eggs,
chicken noodle soup or even mac & cheese
for lunch with a veggie punch!

Old-Fashioned Veggie Soup
Amy Biermann
Riverside, OH

Homestyle taste in half the time!

4 c. beef broth
1-3/4 c. potatoes, peeled
    and diced
1-1/2 c. onion, chopped
1 c. carrot, peeled and sliced
1 c. celery, sliced
1/2 t. dried basil
1/4 t. salt
1/2 t. pepper
1/4 t. dried thyme

2 bay leaves
44-oz. can whole tomatoes,
    undrained
10-oz. pkg. frozen corn, partially
    thawed
10-oz. pkg. frozen baby
    lima beans, partially thawed
10-oz. pkg. frozen sliced okra,
    partially thawed

Combine broth, potatoes, onion, carrot, celery, basil, salt, pepper, thyme and bay leaves together in a large stockpot over medium-high heat. Purée tomatoes in a blender; add to stockpot. Bring to a boil; reduce heat and simmer, covered, for 40 minutes. Add corn and lima beans; simmer and stir occasionally until tender. Add okra; bring to a boil. Reduce heat; simmer for 5 minutes. Discard bay leaves before serving. Serves 8.

Thicken Old-Fashioned Veggie Soup with a sprinkling of instant mashed potato flakes...just right for warming up on a chilly afternoon.

Cheese & Tomato Muffins
May Huffman
Gresham, OR

*My family likes these muffins with scrambled eggs and bacon
in the morning or with creamy tomato soup at lunch.*

2-1/2 c. all-purpose flour
1-1/2 t. baking powder
1/2 t. baking soda
1/2 t. salt
2 T. sugar
1 t. dried basil
2 t. onion, minced
2 eggs, beaten

1 tomato, peeled, seeded
  and chopped
1/2 c. milk
2 T. catsup
1/4 c. butter, melted
3/4 c. shredded Cheddar cheese,
  divided

In a bowl, combine flour, baking powder, baking soda, salt, sugar
and basil; set aside. In a separate bowl, mix onion, eggs, tomato, milk,
catsup and butter; add alternately with 1/2 cup cheese to flour mixture.
Stir until just moistened; fill greased or paper-lined muffin cups
2/3 full. Sprinkle with remaining cheese; bake at 375 degrees until
golden, about 18 minutes. Makes 12.

Serve these muffins as a snack and watch them
disappear! Baked in mini muffin tins,
they're fun for lunch boxes too.

Suzie's Pasta Salad

*Susann Young
Mount Victory, OH*

Make plenty and take the leftovers for lunch...this salad is always better the next day!

12-oz. pkg. tri-color pasta
1 onion, chopped
2 carrots, peeled and chopped
3.8-oz. can sliced black olives, drained
8 cherry tomatoes, chopped

1 green pepper, chopped
5-3/4 oz. jar green olives, drained
16-oz. bottle Italian salad dressing

Cook pasta according to package directions; drain and rinse in cold water. Pour into a large serving bowl. Add remaining ingredients; mix well. Cover and refrigerate until serving. Serves 6 to 8.

Guacamole Salad

*Michael Curry
Ardmore, OK*

Serve as an appetizer with corn chips or croutons.

2 avocados, halved, pitted and chopped
1 tomato, chopped
1 cucumber, peeled and chopped
2 green onions, chopped
2 T. lime juice

1 clove garlic, minced
1/4 t. garlic powder
1 T. dried parsley
3/4 t. salt
1/2 t. pepper
hot pepper sauce to taste

In a large bowl, toss all ingredients together gently. Cover and refrigerate until ready to serve. Serves 4.

White Chicken Pizza

Michelle Schuberg
Big Rapids, MI

A quick & easy dinner even your most finicky eaters will love!

13.8-oz. can refrigerated pizza
    crust dough
1 T. olive oil
2 boneless, skinless chicken
    breasts, cubed
2 T. garlic, minced
15-oz. jar Alfredo pasta sauce

1/2 c. onion, chopped
8-oz. pkg. shredded mozzarella,
    Parmesan & Romano-blend
    cheese

Spread dough onto a lightly greased pizza baking pan; bake at 425 degrees for 7 minutes. Meanwhile, heat oil in a skillet over medium heat. Sauté chicken and garlic until chicken juices run clear when pierced. Spread Alfredo sauce over baked crust; sprinkle with chicken and onion. Bake at 425 degrees for 10 minutes; top with cheese and return to oven for 5 minutes, or until cheese melts. Serves 8.

Use flavored butters to add quick & easy appeal to refrigerated pizza crust...just mix, melt and brush on crust before baking. Try fresh minced herbs, finely chopped onions or grated Parmesan cheese too!

Calico Corn Salsa

Bonnie Weber
West Palm Beach, FL

So fresh and easy to make, serve with tortilla chips.

2 15-oz. cans corn, drained
2 16-oz. cans black beans,
    drained and rinsed
1 green pepper, diced
1 onion, diced
1 bunch arugula, torn

6-oz. can black olives, drained
    and chopped
1 tomato, chopped
8-oz. bottle Italian salad
    dressing
salt and pepper to taste

In a large bowl, combine all ingredients; cover and refrigerate until chilled. Toss gently before serving. Serves 8 to 10.

Granny's Corn Fritters

Kim Anderson
Shiloh, NJ

Great alongside fish fillets or fried chicken.

1 c. corn
1/2 c. milk
1 egg, beaten
1 c. all-purpose flour

1-1/2 t. baking powder
salt to taste
oil for deep frying

In a bowl, mix all ingredients except for oil; set aside. Pour 2 to 3 inches of oil into a heavy saucepan; heat to 365 degrees. Gently drop batter by tablespoonfuls into oil; fry until golden, turning once. Makes 3 to 4 dozen.

Add a pinch of sugar to the water when boiling ears of fresh summer corn...it'll bring out its natural sweetness.

Chicken Taco Salad

Abby Snay
San Francisco, CA

Such a colorful and tasty taco lunch!

8 6-inch flour tortillas
2 c. cooked chicken breast, shredded
2 t. taco seasoning mix
1/2 c. water
2 c. lettuce, shredded
1/2 c. black beans, drained and rinsed

1 c. shredded Cheddar cheese
1/2 c. green onion, sliced
1/2 c. canned corn, drained
2-1/4 oz. can sliced black olives, drained
1/2 avocado, pitted, peeled and cubed
Garnish: fresh salsa

Microwave tortillas on high setting for one minute, or until softened. Press each tortilla into an ungreased muffin cup to form a bowl shape. Bake at 350 degrees for 10 minutes; cool. Combine chicken, taco seasoning and water in a skillet over medium heat. Cook, stirring frequently, until blended, about 5 minutes. Divide lettuce among tortilla bowls. Top with chicken and other ingredients, garnishing with salsa.

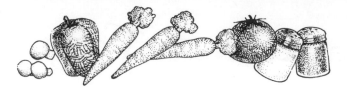

Roasted Onions

Lori Seligman
Schenectady, NY

An easy campfire or grill side dish...just wrap onions up tightly in an aluminum foil packet and turn frequently.

4 sweet onions, peeled
4 T. olive oil
1 t. dried thyme

1/4 t. pepper
1 T. balsamic vinegar

Slice each onion into 8 wedges; arrange flat-side down on a lightly greased 15"x10" jelly-roll pan. Lightly brush olive oil on each wedge; sprinkle with thyme and pepper. Bake, uncovered, at 350 degrees for 30 minutes. Turn onions over; bake an additional 25 minutes. Drizzle with vinegar before serving. Serves 8.

Herbed Artichoke Salad

Michelle Serrano
Ramona, CA

Serve this quick & easy salad in lettuce-lined bowls.

2 T. lemon juice
2 T. olive oil
1 T. sugar
1/8 t. garlic powder
1/4 t. dried tarragon

1/4 t. dried oregano
15-oz. can artichoke hearts,
   drained and chopped
2 c. sliced mushrooms

In a serving bowl, combine lemon juice, olive oil, sugar and seasonings; stir in artichokes and mushrooms. Toss well; cover and refrigerate until serving. Serves 4.

Using fresh artichoke hearts for this recipe? Be sure to only use stainless steel knives and bowls to avoid discoloring them.

Citrus Spinach Salad

Rose Frey
Syracuse, UT

So colorful on the potluck table!

10-oz. pkg. spinach salad mix
15-oz. can mandarin oranges,
    drained

1 c. sliced mushrooms
6 slices bacon, crisply cooked
    and crumbled

Mix all ingredients together in a serving bowl; add Salad Dressing and gently toss. Serve immediately. Serves 6.

Salad Dressing:

1/2 c. oil
3 T. catsup
2 T. cider vinegar
1-1/2 t. Worcestershire sauce

1/4 c. sugar
2 T. onion, finely chopped
1/8 t. salt
pepper to taste

Whisk all ingredients together.

Want a dessert just right for a breezy sunny day? Cut up strawberries, fresh pineapple and cantaloupe...toss with raspberries, grapes and a little sugar. Refrigerate until a light syrup forms and spoon over watermelon wedges to serve!

Yummy Coleslaw

Jill Tatton
Corvallis, MT

Bacon adds extra crunch to this recipe...yum!

3/4 c. mayonnaise-type salad
   dressing
1 T. sugar
8-oz. pkg. coleslaw mix

1/2 c. peanuts, chopped
1/4 c. red cabbage, shredded
4 slices bacon, crisply cooked
   and crumbled

In a serving bowl, combine salad dressing and sugar; mix well. Add remaining ingredients; gently toss. Cover and chill until serving. Serves 4 to 6.

Make-Ahead Onion Salad

Judie Laughlin
Heppner, OR

Just right for those cookin'-out-on-the-grill nights.

1/2 c. water
1 c. vinegar
1 T. sugar
4 sweet onions, thinly sliced

1/4 c. mayonnaise
1-1/2 t. celery seed
1/8 t. salt
1/8 t. pepper

In a bowl, mix water, vinegar and sugar; stir in onions. Cover; refrigerate for 5 hours. Drain and discard marinade; separate onions into rings. In a serving bowl, blend mayonnaise, celery seed, salt and pepper; toss in onions, stirring to coat. Serve chilled. Serves 8.

Make mayo go the extra mile! Flavor it with crushed
garlic, chopped fresh herbs, lemon juice
or even ready-made pesto.

Hoagie Salad

Janet Myers
Reading, PA

This recipe came from my friend, Winnie. Often on my birthday, she includes a favorite recipe in my birthday card. Each time I make one of the yummy dishes, I smile and remember my special friend.

1/2 c. oil
1/4 c. vinegar
dried oregano, salt and pepper
  to taste
16-oz. pkg. elbow macaroni,
  cooked
2 tomatoes, chopped

1 green pepper, chopped
1 onion, chopped
1/2 lb. cooked ham, chopped
1/2 lb. Genoa salami, chopped
1/4 lb. provolone cheese, cubed
1/2 lb. mozzarella cheese, cubed

In a small bowl, whisk oil and vinegar together; add seasonings and set aside. Rinse macaroni in cold water; drain and pour into a large serving bowl. Add remaining ingredients; pour oil and vinegar mixture on top. Toss gently; cover and refrigerate until serving. Makes 10 to 12 servings.

A whole new twist on Hoagie Salad...toss in cooked chicken or turkey breast and sprinkle with fresh parsley.

Stuffed Tomatoes

Stacy Keller
Lee's Summit, MO

Stuffed with chicken salad, these are so yummy
for lunch or a light dinner.

2 tomatoes
10-oz. can chicken, drained
5 green onions, sliced
1 clove garlic, minced

1/3 c. mayonnaise
salt and pepper to taste
2/3 c. shredded mozzarella
  cheese

Slice tomatoes in half; scoop out pulp to make 4 halves. Discard pulp; set aside tomatoes. Flake chicken into a bowl; add onions, garlic, mayonnaise, salt and pepper. Divide and spoon equally into the tomato halves; sprinkle with cheese. Broil for 5 minutes or until warmed through and cheese is golden and bubbly. Makes 4.

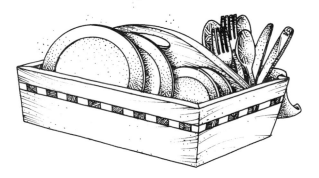

When broiling or baking tomatoes, whole or stuffed, use a muffin tin sprayed with non-stick cooking spray. The tomatoes will sit up straight and hold their shape...so easy!

Gardener's Special Platter

Lisa Miller
Lorain, OH

*This recipe is tasty enough to convince my high school
cooking class that veggies CAN be yummy!*

4 c. broccoli flowerets	1/2 t. garlic salt
1-1/2 c. cauliflower flowerets	1/4 t. fresh thyme, chopped
1 zucchini, sliced	1 tomato
3 T. margarine	1/4 c. grated Parmesan cheese

Arrange broccoli flowerets toward the edge of a 12" glass serving
plate with floweret ends facing the outer edge. Arrange cauliflower
flowerets between broccoli. Mound zucchini in center of plate. Cover
entire plate with plastic wrap, pricking tiny holes into wrap. Microwave
on medium setting for 9 to 11 minutes or until vegetables are just
tender; set aside. Melt margarine in a small saucepan; stir in garlic salt
and thyme. Remove from heat; set aside. Slice tomato into 8 wedges;
remove plastic wrap from vegetable plate and arrange wedges on top.
Drizzle with margarine mixture; sprinkle with Parmesan cheese.
Microwave, uncovered, for 1-1/2 to 2 minutes on medium, until
tomatoes are heated through. Serves 8 to 10.

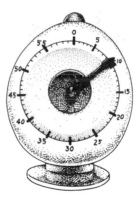

It's difficult to think anything but pleasant thoughts
while eating a homegrown tomato.

–Lewis Grizzard

Easy Potato Casserole

Raye Polin
North Charleston, SC

*Serve alongside scrambled eggs in the morning
or meatloaf at dinner.*

2-lb. pkg. frozen shredded
    hashbrowns, thawed
2 c. sour cream
10-3/4 oz. can cream of
    celery soup
1 c. shredded sharp Cheddar
    cheese

1/2 c. butter, melted
1 t. salt
1 t. pepper
1/4 c. onion, minced
1/3 c. milk
1/2 c. round buttery crackers,
    crushed

Combine all ingredients except crackers; spoon into a lightly greased
13"x9" baking pan. Sprinkle crackers on top. Bake, uncovered, at
350 degrees until bubbly, about 40 minutes. Serves 6 to 8.

Make this casserole the night before and bake it alongside
Easy Mini Meatloaves (on page 99). A simple salad
completes this dinner in minutes!

Veggie Bagel

Jodel Guerrero
Fresno, CA

A cool sandwich that packs well for lunches on warm days.

4 to 6 T. cream cheese, softened
1 bagel, sliced horizontally
1-1/2 T. roasted sunflower seeds
1 cucumber, sliced
1 tomato, sliced
1 leaf romaine lettuce
alfalfa sprouts to taste

Spread cream cheese evenly on each bagel half; sprinkle with sunflower seeds. Layer with desired amount of cucumber and tomato slices; add lettuce leaf and alfalfa sprouts. Top with remaining bagel half. Makes one sandwich.

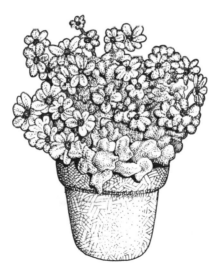

Easy lunchbox dippers! Wrap sliced apples and send along a cup of peanut butter for dipping. Try packing salsa, cream cheese or creamy salad dressing for dipping celery or carrot sticks.

Vegetable Bake

Glory Bock
Lee's Summit, MO

*My Italian son-in-law first made this dish for our family
on Thanksgiving...we love it!*

13-1/4 oz. can mushroom
   pieces, drained
1 onion, diced
1/4 c. butter
10-3/4 oz. can cream of
   mushroom soup
10-3/4 oz. can cream of
   chicken soup
11-oz. can cut green beans,
   drained

11-oz. can yellow wax beans,
   drained
11-oz. can sliced carrots,
   drained
8-oz. pkg. shredded Cheddar
   cheese
8-oz. pkg. shredded mozzarella
   cheese

In a large skillet over medium heat, sauté mushrooms and onion in
butter until tender; add soups, beans and carrots. Remove from heat;
spread into a lightly greased 13"x9" baking pan. Combine cheeses;
sprinkle on top. Bake, uncovered, at 350 degrees until bubbly, about
30 minutes. Makes 12 to 15 servings.

Cutting up veggies for dinner? Go ahead and cut up some
extra for lunch the next day. Save time in the morning
and clean up once instead of twice!

Garlic-Herb Mushrooms

Tina Stidam
Delaware, OH

*Great as a side dish, over chicken, baked potatoes,
with brown rice or added to casseroles.*

1/2 c. olive oil
3 cloves garlic, minced
4 c. mushrooms, whole or
  thickly sliced
2 T. fresh parsley, chopped

3 green onions, finely chopped
1 T. white wine or chicken broth
garlic powder to taste
1/3 c. grated Parmesan cheese

Heat oil in a skillet; sauté garlic and mushrooms until tender. Add parsley and onions; stir constantly. Pour in wine or broth; simmer for 4 minutes. Spread in a lightly greased 1-1/2 quart casserole dish; top with Whole-Wheat Croutons. Sprinkle with garlic powder and Parmesan cheese. Bake, uncovered, at 350 degrees for 10 to 15 minutes; serve warm. Serves 4.

Whole-Wheat Croutons:

3 slices whole-wheat bread
2 cloves garlic, minced
3 T. olive oil

2 t. grated Parmesan cheese
1 t. dried parsley

Cut bread into one-inch cubes; sauté with garlic in olive oil. Sprinkle with cheese and parsley; heat until golden, stirring constantly.

Use mini cookie cutters to cut bread and create whimsical croutons...tiny leaves make a harvest dinner fun.

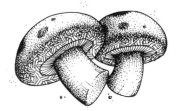

Garlic Deviled Eggs

Jennifer Stout
Blandon, PA

*Serve these eggs at your next potluck or picnic and
guests will be pleasantly surprised!*

6 eggs, hard-boiled and peeled
1/3 c. mayonnaise
1/2 to 1 t. mustard
1 t. pickle relish

1 onion, chopped
1 clove garlic, minced
1/8 t. salt
Garnish: paprika

Slice eggs in half lengthwise; remove yolks, setting egg whites aside.
In a bowl, combine yolks, mayonnaise, mustard, relish, onion, garlic
and salt; mix well. Fill egg whites with mixture; sprinkle with paprika.
Makes 12.

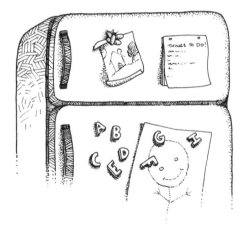

Making deviled eggs for an afternoon picnic?
Whip 'em up in no time by combining ingredients in
a plastic zipping bag instead of a bowl. Blend by
squeezing the bag, snip off a corner and pipe
the filling into the whites...what could be easier?

Amish Skillet

*Sandy Sell
Woodburn, IN*

A tasty comfort food that'll be welcome year 'round.

1 lb. ground beef, browned
1 c. potatoes, peeled and sliced
1 c. carrot, peeled and sliced
1/2 c. onion, sliced

10-3/4 oz. can cream of
   mushroom soup
8-oz. pkg. shredded Cheddar
   cheese

Spread beef in a skillet; layer potatoes, carrot and onion on top. Spoon soup over top; sprinkle with cheese. Cover and simmer over low heat until vegetables are tender, about 30 minutes. Makes 4 to 6 servings.

Zucchini Pie

*Ginny Paccioretti
Oak Ridge, NJ*

An inside-out pie...the crust is baked right in with the filling!

1 c. biscuit baking mix
4 eggs, beaten
1/4 c. oil
1/2 c. grated Parmesan cheese
salt and pepper to taste

4 c. zucchini, sliced and
   quartered
1 onion, diced
1 clove garlic, chopped

In a bowl, combine baking mix, eggs, oil, Parmesan cheese, salt and pepper; stir in vegetables. Spread into a lightly greased13"x9" baking pan. Bake, uncovered, at 350 degrees for 45 minutes. Serves 6 to 8.

Munch on kabobs after school...skewer fresh
veggies and cubes of cheese on toothpicks
and make snacktime fun!

Beefy Mushroom Soup

Jackie Sampson
Central City, NE

A quick soup we enjoy with grilled cheese sandwiches.

8-oz. pkg. sliced mushrooms
1 onion, diced
1/4 c. butter, melted
1/4 c. all-purpose flour
1 c. beef broth

2 c. half-and-half, warmed
salt and pepper to taste
1/4 t. nutmeg
1 bay leaf

In a skillet over medium heat, sauté mushrooms and onion in butter until golden. Whisk in flour, mixing well. Slowly add broth; stir constantly until thickened. Reduce heat; add half-and-half. Stir in seasonings; heat over low heat for 10 minutes. Do not allow to boil. Remove bay leaf before serving. Serves 4 to 6.

Only the pure of heart can make good soup.
–Beethoven

⋆ **Market Fresh** & Fast ⋆

Olivia Salad

Sharon Pettit
Duluth, MN

We like it refrigerated overnight.

3/4 c. mayonnaise
1/2 c. sour cream
salt and pepper to taste
6 potatoes, peeled, boiled and
    cubed
15-1/4 oz. can peas, drained

2 sweet pickles, chopped
4 to 5 green onions, sliced
4 eggs, hard-boiled, peeled
    and sliced
1 lb. Kielbasa sausage, cubed
    and browned

In a serving bowl, combine all ingredients; toss gently. Cover and refrigerate until serving. Makes 8 to 10 servings.

Broccoli-Cheese Squares

Julie Wise
Delaware, OH

Simply delicious as a side or an appetizer.

3 T. butter
3 eggs, beaten
1 c. milk
1 c. all-purpose flour
1 t. baking powder

2 10-oz. pkgs. frozen chopped
    broccoli, steamed and
    drained
1/4 c. onion, chopped
4 c. shredded Cheddar cheese

Melt butter in a 13"x9" baking pan; tilt to coat the bottom and set aside. In a bowl, mix eggs, milk, flour and baking powder; fold in broccoli, onion and cheese. Spread into pan; bake, uncovered, at 350 degrees for 30 to 35 minutes. Cut into squares to serve. Makes 12 to 15 servings.

Tangy Almond Salad

Kelly Summey
Stanley, NC

Sweet and savory, this salad is one of our favorites.

1 head lettuce, torn
2 11-oz. cans mandarin
   oranges, drained
1/8 c. sliced almonds, toasted
1/2 c. oil
1/2 c. sugar

1/2 c. cider vinegar
1 t. Worcestershire sauce
1-1/2 T. onion, minced
1-1/2 T. sesame seed
1-1/2 T. poppy seed

In a large serving bowl, toss lettuce, oranges and almonds; set aside. In a separate bowl, whisk together remaining ingredients; pour over lettuce mixture. Toss to coat. Serve immediately. Serves 6.

Creamy Fruit Salad

Wendy Azevedo
Chico, CA

Take the recipe along whenever you take this salad to potlucks and picnics...it's sure to be requested!

20-oz. can pineapple chunks,
   drained
15-oz. can sliced peaches,
   drained
11-oz. can mandarin oranges,
   drained
4 apples, cored, peeled and diced

1-1/2 c. milk
1/3 c. frozen orange juice
   concentrate, thawed
3.4-oz. pkg. instant vanilla
   pudding mix
3/4 c. sour cream

Combine fruit in a large serving bowl; set aside. In a separate bowl, whisk milk, orange juice and dry pudding mix together until smooth; stir in sour cream. Fold into fruit mixture. Cover and refrigerate until serving. Serves 16.

Frosty Fruit Salad

Lisa Smith
Littleton, CO

Made the night before, it's just right for afternoon picnics!

17-oz. can apricots, chopped and
    juice reserved
17-oz. can crushed pineapple,
    juice reserved
1/2 c. sugar
3 10-oz. pkgs. frozen
    strawberries, thawed

6-oz. can frozen orange
    juice concentrate
2 T. lemon juice
2 lbs. grapes, halved
4 bananas, diced

In a large heavy saucepan over medium heat, cook reserved juices and sugar until sugar dissolves. Add strawberries, orange juice and lemon juice. Heat until warmed; remove from heat. Combine apricots, pineapple, grapes and bananas; add to contents of the saucepan. Mix well. Pour into a freezer-proof serving dish; freeze overnight. Remove from freezer about 15 to 25 minutes before serving. Serves 25 to 30.

Roll some fresh grapes, strawberries and mandarin oranges in extra-fine sugar for a glittery (and tasty!) garnish.

Spicy Salsa Shrimp

Cheryl Anthony
Camden, DE

A dish that is bursting with flavors...try it served over pasta or rice!

18-oz. pkg. frozen shrimp,
    thawed
2 cloves garlic, minced
1 T. oil

3/4 c. salsa
1/4 c. fresh cilantro, chopped
1-1/2 c. shredded Mexican
    cheese blend

Peel and devein shrimp; sauté shrimp and garlic in oil in a skillet over medium heat for 4 minutes. Stir in salsa. Remove from heat; add cilantro. Pour into an ungreased 2-quart casserole dish; sprinkle with cheese. Bake, uncovered, at 350 degrees for 10 minutes or until golden. Serves 4.

Cajun Shrimp Curry

Ann Mathis
Biscoe, AR

Whip up this yummy seafood dish and warm up
your family's tummies.

1/2 c. butter
1 onion, diced
3 stalks celery, diced
1 green pepper, diced
2 10-3/4 oz. cans cream of
    celery soup

1 c. milk
2 lbs. shrimp, cleaned and
    cooked
salt, pepper and curry powder
    to taste
cooked rice

Melt butter in a Dutch oven over medium heat; sauté onion, celery and green pepper until tender. Mix in soup and milk; warm thoroughly. Fold in shrimp; season with salt, pepper and curry powder. Simmer until warmed through; spoon over warm rice. Makes 4 servings.

Colorful Couscous Salad

Donna Cash
Dexter, MI

Look for flavored couscous in the pasta aisle...so tasty and easy!

10-oz. box couscous
3/4 c. olive oil
1/4 c. lemon juice
1/8 c. white wine vinegar
2 T. sugar
1 T. garlic, minced
3 drops hot pepper sauce
1/2 t. salt
1/2 t. pepper
1/2 t. lemon pepper

1/2 t. seasoned salt
1/4 t. turmeric
1/8 t. cinnamon
1/8 t. ground ginger
1 green pepper, diced
1 bunch green onions, diced
4 carrots, shredded
15-1/4 oz. can corn, drained
15-1/2 oz. can black beans,
    drained and rinsed

Prepare couscous according to package directions; drain and set aside.
In a large serving bowl, whisk olive oil, lemon juice, vinegar, sugar
and seasonings; stir in vegetables and beans. Add couscous, mixing
well. Cover and refrigerate until serving. Makes 6 to 8 servings.

Serve up individual servings of this colorful dish in
edible bowls! Hollow out fresh green or red peppers
and fill 'em up for a quick and tasty lunch.

French Onion Casserole

Karla Edmonson
Gracey, KY

Sprinkle extra croutons on top for added crunch.

4 sweet onions, sliced
5 T. butter, melted and divided
2 T. all-purpose flour
salt and pepper to taste

1 c. beef broth
1-1/2 c. croutons
1/2 c. shredded Swiss cheese
3 T. grated Parmesan cheese

In a skillet over medium heat, sauté onions in 3 tablespoons butter until tender; stir in flour, salt, pepper and broth. Cook and stir until thickened; remove from heat. Spread in an ungreased 1-1/2 quart casserole dish. Toss croutons with remaining butter; spoon over onion mixture. Sprinkle with cheeses; place under a broiler for one minute, or until cheese melts. Serves 4 to 6.

Carrot Casserole

Beth McCarthy
Nashua, NH

Top with bread crumbs, if you like.

2/3 c. pasteurized process
   cheese spread, cubed
2 T. butter

1 T. dried, minced onion
2 lbs. carrots, peeled, cooked
   and mashed

Melt cheese and butter in a double boiler; add onion and carrots, mixing well. Spread in a lightly greased 13"x9" baking pan. Bake, uncovered, at 350 degrees for 15 to 20 minutes. Serves 6 to 8.

Sweet Potato Casserole

Dawn Romero
Lewisville, TX

This is great to take to holiday parties or gatherings.

4 c. mashed sweet potatoes
1/3 c. plus 2 T. butter, melted
  and divided
2 T. sugar
2 eggs, beaten

1/2 c. milk
1/3 c. chopped pecans
1/3 c. sweetened flaked coconut
1/3 c. brown sugar, packed
2 T. all-purpose flour

In a large bowl, mix together sweet potatoes, 1/3 cup butter and sugar. Stir in eggs and milk. Spoon mixture into a lightly greased 2-quart casserole dish. In a separate bowl, combine remaining butter and other ingredients. Sprinkle mixture over sweet potatoes. Bake, uncovered, at 325 degrees for one hour, or until heated through and bubbly. Serves 4.

Arrange a ring of large marshmallows around the edge
of a baking pan full of sweet potatoes. Bake as usual
until marshmallows are golden and bubbly.
A sweet treat...just watch 'em disappear!

Cheesy Potato Bake

Shari Miller
Hobart, IN

*Stir in cooked, diced ham before baking, add a fresh salad
on the side and you've got a complete meal!*

4 potatoes, peeled and thinly
   sliced
1/4 c. butter
1 T. onion, minced
1 t. salt

1/2 t. dried thyme
1/8 t. pepper
1 c. shredded Cheddar cheese
1 T. fresh parsley, chopped

Arrange potatoes in a greased 2-quart casserole dish; set aside. Melt butter in a saucepan over low heat; add onion, salt, thyme and pepper, stirring until onion is tender. Drizzle over potatoes; cover and bake at 425 degrees for 45 minutes. Sprinkle with cheese and parsley; bake, uncovered, for an additional 15 minutes. Serves 6.

Southwest Salad Twist

Deborah Thorpe
Tucson, AZ

A colorful cold salad...looks and tastes delicious.

1 c. frozen corn, thawed
15-oz. can black beans, drained
   and rinsed
3 to 4 tomatoes, finely chopped

1/4 c. green onions, chopped
1/4 c. fresh cilantro, chopped
1 T. chopped green chiles
juice of 1 to 2 limes

In a bowl, combine all ingredients except lime juice; mix well. Drizzle with lime juice; gently stir. Chill before serving. Serves 4 to 6.

Quick & Easy Veggie Soup

Valerie Pierce
Peach Bottom, PA

Unexpected company dropping in? Just add some more veggies for plenty of hearty soup.

1 lb. ground beef
1 onion, diced
4 carrots, peeled and chopped
4 potatoes, peeled and chopped
1 c. pearled barley, uncooked

6 beef bouillon cubes
6 c. water
28-oz. can tomato purée
1 t. dried thyme

In a skillet over medium heat, brown beef and onion until beef is no longer pink; drain. Transfer beef mixture and remaining ingredients to a large stockpot; bring to a boil. Reduce heat; simmer until vegetables are tender, about 45 minutes. Stir occasionally; add water while simmering to thin consistency, as desired. Makes 6 to 8 servings.

Look for bulk bags of frozen corn at the grocery store and split the bag up into individual or dinner-size portions. Store in plastic zipping bags for a super speedy side dish.

Broccoli Salad

Debbie Bymers
Tacoma, WA

A cheesy twist on an old favorite.

1/2 c. mayonnaise
1/4 c. sugar
2 T. vinegar
1 head broccoli, chopped

1 sweet onion, diced
1 c. shredded Cheddar cheese
6 to 8 slices bacon, crisply
   cooked and crumbled

In a small bowl, whisk together mayonnaise, sugar and vinegar; set aside. In a serving bowl, combine broccoli, onion, cheese and bacon; pour mayonnaise mixture over the top, tossing gently. Serve immediately. Makes 6 to 8 servings.

Try adding cauliflower, carrots or green pepper
to this classic salad...the more veggies, the better!

Ziti-Veggie Salad

Vickie
Gooseberry Patch

This is a perfect pasta salad for potlucks!

16-oz. pkg. ziti pasta
1 c. cooked asparagus, chopped
15-oz. can baby corn, drained
1/2 c. oil-packed sun-dried
   tomatoes, diced

2 T. fresh parsley, chopped
2 T. fresh basil, chopped
1/2 c. Italian or Caesar salad
   dressing

Cook pasta according to package directions; drain and rinse in cold water. In a large serving bowl, toss pasta with vegetables and herbs. Add dressing and toss to coat. Chill before serving. Serves 4.

Combine the ingredients for a simple salad dressing
in a squeeze bottle instead of a bowl. Shake bottle to
incorporate flavors and squirt onto
salad…what could be easier?

Oodles of Noodles

Chicken & Bowties

Rosalia Henry
Hyde Park, NY

Fresh and ready in a flash!

16-oz. pkg. bowtie pasta
1 bunch asparagus, trimmed and
   coarsely chopped
1 lb. chicken breasts, cooked
   and chopped

1/2 c. grated Parmesan
   cheese
2 T. dried parsley
1/4 c. olive oil

Prepare pasta according to directions on package; add asparagus
for the last one to 2 minutes of cooking time. Drain. Place pasta,
asparagus and chicken in a lightly greased 13"x9" baking pan; mix
in remaining ingredients. Broil for 5 minutes, or until top is crisp.
Serves 6.

Cooking pasta or rice for dinner? Toss in a few eggs to
hard-boil while it's cooking and, while dinner's baking,
whip up some tasty egg salad for tomorrow's lunch!

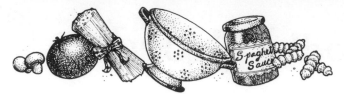

Garden Macaroni Salad

Susan Brzozowski
Ellicott City, MD

This salad is good anytime but we love it in the summertime!

1 c. mayonnaise
2 T. cider vinegar
2 T. fresh dill, chopped
1/4 t. salt
1/8 t. pepper
8-oz. pkg. elbow macaroni,
    cooked

1 c. cucumber, peeled and
    chopped
1 c. cherry tomatoes, quartered
1/4 c. green onions, sliced

Combine mayonnaise, vinegar, dill, salt and pepper in a large serving bowl; set aside. Rinse macaroni in cold water; drain. Add to mayonnaise mixture; stir in remaining ingredients. Cover; refrigerate until serving. Serves 6.

Packing this salad for a picnic or in lunch boxes? Freeze a few juice boxes and they'll keep the whole lunch cool!

Carolyn's Chicken Tetrazzi

Carolyn Knight
Oklahoma City, OK

Scrumptious made with leftover holiday turkey too.

2 c. sliced mushrooms
1/4 c. butter
3 T. all-purpose flour
2 c. chicken broth
1/4 c. light cream
3 T. sherry or chicken broth
1 T. fresh parsley, chopped

1 t. salt
1/8 t. pepper
1/8 t. nutmeg
3 c. cooked chicken, cubed
8-oz. pkg. spaghetti, cooked
1 c. grated Parmesan cheese

In a Dutch oven over medium heat, sauté mushrooms in butter until tender. Stir in flour. Add chicken broth; cook, stirring constantly, until sauce is thickened. Remove from heat; stir in cream, sherry or broth and seasonings. Fold in chicken and cooked spaghetti; turn mixture into a lightly greased 13"x9" baking pan. Sprinkle with Parmesan cheese. Cool; cover with aluminum foil and freeze, or bake at 350 degrees for 30 to 35 minutes, until heated through. Let stand for 5 to 10 minutes. Serves 8.

Mushrooms absorb water like a sponge. Instead of washing mushrooms under a faucet, just wipe them off with a damp cloth...they'll stay firm and yummy!

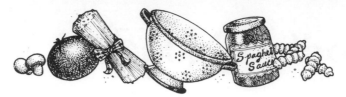

Pesto Linguine

Brian Harple
Grandview, OH

It's fast, it's tasty, it's a winner!

16-oz. pkg. linguine
.67-oz. pkg. fresh basil
1 c. olive oil

3 cloves garlic, pressed
1/4 c. grated Romano cheese

Prepare linguine according to package directions; drain and transfer to a large serving bowl. Combine basil, olive oil, garlic and cheese in a food processor; blend on high. Add basil mixture to linguine. Mix well and serve immediately. Makes 6 to 8 servings.

Serve an Italian feast! This simple pesto makes a
hearty appetizer when spread on crusty bread...top
cooked linguine with a ready-made Alfredo sauce
and whip up a crisp green salad.

Oodles of Noodles

Creamy Chicken Spaghetti

Aimee Bowlin
Keithville, LA

This is one of my husband's favorite meals, and I enjoy making it since it's so quick & easy!

2 lbs. chicken breasts, cooked
  and shredded
16-oz. pkg. spaghetti, cooked
2 14-1/2 oz. cans stewed
  tomatoes, chopped
2 10-3/4 oz. cans cream of
  chicken soup

10-3/4 oz. can cream of
  mushroom soup
4-oz. can mushrooms, drained
8-oz. pkg. pasteurized process
  cheese spread, cubed

Combine all ingredients in a Dutch oven; cook over medium heat until warmed through and cheese is melted. Serves 8.

Chicken & Noodles

Laura Cottrell
Payne, OH

A sure-fire shortcut to a family favorite.

8-oz. pkg. medium egg noodles,
  cooked
3 10-3/4 oz. cans cream of
  chicken soup

16-oz. can chicken broth
6-1/2 oz. can chicken

Combine all ingredients in a large saucepan; cook over medium heat until mixture reaches desired consistency. Makes 4 to 6 servings.

There are endless possibilities with Chicken & Noodles!
Add whatever fresh veggies are handy or sprinkle
with cheese for a twist.

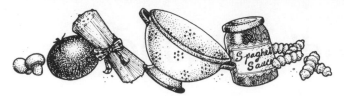

Zesty Primavera Pasta

Rachel Shelton
Franklin, OH

Pick your favorites from the garden to add to this delicious dish.

1 c. zucchini, peeled and
    chopped
1 c. red pepper, chopped
1 c. yellow squash, peeled
    and chopped
1 c. carrot, peeled and chopped
1 c. eggplant, peeled and
    chopped

6 T. honey mustard, divided
3 T. olive oil
2 T. cider vinegar
1 T. fresh basil, chopped
8-oz. pkg. penne pasta, cooked

In a 15"x10" jelly-roll pan, toss vegetables with 4 tablespoons mustard; broil until tender and set aside. Whisk remaining mustard, olive oil, vinegar and basil together in a serving bowl; add pasta, stirring gently. Fold in vegetables, tossing lightly until well coated. Serves 6.

When freezing leftover diced peppers, corn or fresh herbs, add a little olive oil to the plastic zipping bag and shake. The oil will help keep the food separate and fresher too. They'll be ready to drop into sauces, salsas and salads!

Oodles of Noodles

Vermicelli with Shrimp

Kim Gludt
Anaheim, CA

No shrimp on hand? Cooked chicken works well in this recipe too!

12-oz. pkg. vermicelli pasta
1 onion, chopped
2 T. oil
2 cloves garlic, minced
16-oz. can crushed tomatoes in
   thick purée

1/4 t. red pepper flakes
3/4 t. salt
1 lb. shrimp, cleaned and cooked

Prepare pasta according to package directions; drain and keep warm. In a skillet over medium heat, sauté onion in oil until tender, about 5 minutes. Add garlic, stirring 30 seconds more. Mix in tomatoes, red pepper flakes and salt; reduce heat and simmer for 10 minutes. Add shrimp, stirring until warmed through, about 4 minutes. Pour sauce over warm pasta; stir gently to mix. Makes 4 to 6 servings.

Salmon & Shell Salad

Patricia Thomas
San Antonio, TX

A layered salad just right for picnics and potlucks.

8-oz. pkg. small shell pasta
4 c. shredded lettuce
2 c. tomatoes, chopped
15-oz. can salmon, drained

1-1/2 c. mayonnaise
2 T. milk
1/4 c. green onions, chopped
1/2 t. dill weed

Prepare pasta according to package directions; drain. In a 3-quart casserole dish, layer lettuce, pasta, tomatoes and salmon; chill until serving time. In a small bowl, combine remaining ingredients; refrigerate until chilled. Pour over salmon before serving. Serves 6 to 8.

Overnight Oriental Salad

Michelle Allman
Seymour, IN

For the crunchiest salad, toss with dressing
just before serving!

3/4 c. oil
1/2 c. sugar
1/2 c. white vinegar
2 3-oz. pkgs. Oriental ramen
    noodles with seasoning
    packets

1 head cabbage, shredded
1 bunch green onions, chopped
1 c. sliced almonds, toasted
1 c. roasted sunflower seeds

In a bowl, mix oil, sugar, vinegar and seasoning packets from ramen noodles; refrigerate overnight. Crush uncooked ramen noodles in a serving bowl; add cabbage, onions, almonds and sunflower seeds. Pour oil mixture over the top; toss gently. Makes 10 to 12 servings.

Set up a fruit salad bar on the kitchen counter and add some fun to dinnertime. Bowls of fresh strawberries, blueberries, grapes, kiwi, sliced apples and bananas along with some sweet and creamy fruit dip are yummy additions.

Easy Cheesy Manicotti

Robin Argyle
Kalkaska, MI

*This dish freezes well. Why not make 2 and
freeze one for another night?*

12-oz. pkg. manicotti shells,
  uncooked
1 T. olive oil
1-1/2 t. salt, divided
8-oz. pkg. cream cheese,
  softened
2 c. cottage cheese
12-oz. pkg. shredded Monterey
  Jack cheese

12-oz. pkg. shredded mozzarella
  cheese, divided
1 egg, beaten
1 T. fresh parsley, chopped
1 clove garlic, minced
24-oz. jar spaghetti sauce,
  divided
Optional: chopped fresh parsley

Cook manicotti according to package directions, adding oil and one teaspoon salt; drain and set aside. Meanwhile, combine cream cheese, cottage cheese, Monterey Jack cheese, 2/3 of mozzarella cheese, egg, parsley, garlic and remaining salt; set aside. Spread a thin layer of spaghetti sauce in the bottom of an ungreased 13"x9" baking pan. Spoon cheese filling into each manicotti, filling 3/4 full; arrange on top of sauce. Spoon remaining sauce over manicotti. Bake, uncovered, at 350 degrees for 30 to 45 minutes. Top with remaining mozzarella cheese 10 minutes before done. Let stand minutes before serving. Garnish with additional parsley, if desired. Serves 6.

No-mess manicotti! Instead of a spoon, use a pastry bag to fill cooked pasta shells... they'll be ready in no time.

Monterey Bread

Rita Welters
Bellingham, WA

A tasty side with any pasta dish!

1 c. mayonnaise	1/4 c. grated Parmesan cheese
1/2 c. butter, softened	1 clove garlic, minced
1 c. shredded mild Cheddar cheese	3 green onions, chopped 1 loaf French bread

In a bowl, combine mayonnaise, butter, cheeses, garlic and onions; mix well. Slice French bread in half horizontally; spread mayonnaise mixture thickly on each half. Bake, uncovered, at 375 degrees until golden, about 10 to 15 minutes. Slice to serve. Makes 16 servings.

Instead of buying a pre-baked loaf, try using refrigerated bread dough to make fresh-baked Monterey Bread.

Oodles of Noodles

Cajun Chicken Pasta

Jennifer Boyer
Sidney, MT

A very simple recipe that's big on taste!

3 to 4 boneless, skinless chicken
    breasts, cut into strips
2 t. Cajun seasoning
2 T. butter
8 slices green pepper
8 slices red pepper
4 mushrooms, sliced
2 green onions, sliced
2 c. whipping cream

1/4 t. dried basil
1/4 t. lemon pepper
1/4 t. salt
1/8 t. garlic salt
1/8 t. pepper
8-oz. pkg. linguine, cooked
Garnish: grated Parmesan
    cheese

In a bowl, toss chicken strips with Cajun seasoning. In a skillet over medium heat, sauté chicken in butter about 5 minutes, until fully cooked, about 5 minutes or until juices run clear when pierced with a fork. Add peppers, mushrooms and onions; sauté for 2 to 3 minutes. Reduce heat; add cream and remaining seasonings. Heat through but do not boil. Toss with linguine or spoon over individual servings of linguine. Garnish with Parmesan cheese. Serves 4 to 6.

Put dinner on the to-do list and resist the urge to answer phone messages or read the mail. Focusing on the task at hand will help make meal prep faster and easier too!

Zesty Macaroni & Cheese

Jen Licon-Conner
Gooseberry Patch

Make this recipe extra zesty...add 1/2 cup salsa or stir in green chiles to your taste!

16-oz. pkg. elbow macaroni, cooked
16-oz. pkg. pasteurized processed cheese, cubed

8-oz. pkg. Pepper Jack cheese, cubed
2 10-3/4 oz. cans Cheddar cheese soup
1 c. onion, minced

Place macaroni and cheeses into a slow cooker. Add soup and stir until coated well; add onion. Cover and cook on low setting for 5 to 6 hours, or on high setting for 2 hours. Stir occasionally. Makes 6 to 8 servings.

Pack a little something extra in those brown bags and they'll look forward to lunch. Include some fun stickers, a new pencil or a note to let them know that they're the apple of your eye...you'll make any kid's day!

Lip-Smackin' Stuffed Shells *Nancy Swindle*
Winnemucca, NV

For the creamiest filling, be sure to squeeze all the
water out of the spinach.

12-oz. pkg. jumbo shell pasta
16-oz. pkg. shredded mozzarella
  cheese
2 c. cottage cheese
15-oz. can tomato sauce
2 10-oz. pkgs. frozen chopped
  spinach, thawed and drained

2 eggs, beaten
1/8 t. nutmeg
salt and pepper to taste
28-oz. jar spaghetti sauce,
  divided
Garnish: grated Parmesan
  cheese

Prepare pasta according to package directions; drain and rinse with
cold water. Set aside. In a bowl, combine remaining ingredients except
spaghetti sauce and Parmesan cheese; mix well and set aside. Spread
1/4 cup spaghetti sauce evenly in an ungreased 13"x9" baking pan.
Spoon cheese mixture into shells; arrange stuffed-side up on top of
spaghetti sauce. Pour remaining sauce over the shells; sprinkle with
Parmesan cheese. Bake, uncovered, at 350 degrees for 30 minutes.
Serves 10 to 12.

Cook and chill noodles for filled pasta dishes in advance.
It'll be so much easier to fill shells and recipes
will have one less step.

Mozzarella Sticks

Shari Miller
Hobart, IN

Having company? Make this appetizer the night before and pop it in the oven when guests arrive for quick munchies!

2 eggs, beaten
1 T. water
1 c. bread crumbs
2-1/2 t. Italian seasoning
1/2 t. garlic powder

1/8 t. pepper
12 string cheese sticks
3 T. all-purpose flour
1 T. butter, melted

Whisk eggs and water together in a small bowl; set aside. Combine bread crumbs, Italian seasoning, garlic powder and pepper in a plastic zipping bag; set aside. Coat cheese sticks in flour; dip in egg mixture, then shake in bread crumb mixture. Cover; refrigerate for 4 hours. Arrange on an ungreased baking sheet; drizzle with butter. Bake at 400 degrees for 6 to 8 minutes. Let cool for 3 to 5 minutes before serving. Makes 12.

Have appetizers for dinner! Set up a family-size sampler with these Mozzarella Sticks, mini pizza snacks, mini egg rolls, potato skins and a bunch of dippers to try too. Don't forget the French fries!

Oodles of Noodles

BLT Pasta Salad

Ronda Sierra
Anaheim, CA

Look for pre-shredded lettuce in the
produce aisle...what a time-saver!

8-oz. pkg. elbow macaroni
4 c. tomatoes, peeled, seeded
   and chopped
4 slices bacon, crisply cooked
   and crumbled
3 c. shredded lettuce
1/2 c. mayonnaise

1/3 c. sour cream
1 T. Dijon mustard
1 t. sugar
2 t. cider vinegar
1/2 t. salt
1/2 t. pepper

Prepare macaroni according to package directions; drain and rinse in cold water. Transfer to a serving bowl. Add tomatoes, bacon and lettuce; toss gently and set aside. In a separate bowl, mix remaining ingredients; stir well. Pour over macaroni mixture; gently toss until well coated. Serve immediately. Makes 10 servings.

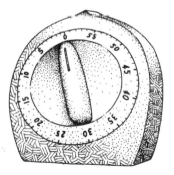

Rub the inside of salad bowls with a halved clove of
garlic...it'll add a hint of flavor to any salad.

Cucumber & Tomato Salad *LaVerne Fang*
Joliet, IL

Add more or less Italian salad dressing to suit your taste.

16-oz. pkg. spaghetti
1 cucumber, peeled and diced
1 tomato, diced
1 sweet onion, diced

1/4 c. salad seasoning
8-oz. bottle Italian salad
   dressing

Prepare pasta according to package directons; drain and rinse in cold water. Transfer to a serving bowl; add vegetables and seasoning. Mix gently. Stir in desired amount of salad dressing. Cover and refrigerate before serving. Makes 10 to 12 servings.

Create homemade salad seasoning and store in the fridge for tasty salads anytime. Combine 2 tablespoons Romano cheese, 1-1/2 teaspoons sesame seed, 1 teaspoon paprika, 1/2 teaspoon salt, 1/4 teaspoon poppy seed, 1/2 teaspoon celery seed, 1/2 teaspoon garlic powder, 1/2 teaspoon coarse pepper and a dash cayenne pepper…keep in a shaker bottle.

Oodles of Noodles

Red & White Harvest Pasta
Chad Rutan
Gooseberry Patch

This farm-fresh pasta is perfect for any get-together...
serve warm or chilled!

8-oz. pkg. fettuccine pasta
4 red peppers, chopped
1/2 c. balsamic vinegar
1 t. garlic, minced
1/4 c. olive oil

2 T. fresh basil, chopped
1 T. fresh oregano, chopped
2 t. red pepper flakes
1/2 c. fresh parsley, chopped

Cook pasta according to package directions; drain. Meanwhile, in a
food processor, purée red peppers with vinegar until smooth. In a
skillet over medium heat, sauté garlic in olive oil; stir in basil, oregano
and pepper flakes. Add pepper purée to skillet and heat through. Stir in
parsley just before serving. Serve over pasta. Serves 4.

Crazy for artichokes? Serve up a side of
Herbed Artichoke Salad. Find it on page 24.

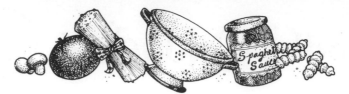

Lemony Angel Hair Pasta

Jo Ann
Gooseberry Patch

This pasta is fabulously fresh...it's my favorite way to use the homegrown grape tomatoes and herbs from my garden!

12-oz. pkg. angel hair pasta
1/2 c. pine nuts
1/4 c. olive oil
3 cloves garlic, minced
2 T. lemon zest

1/4 c. lemon juice
2 c. grape tomatoes, halved
1/4 c. fresh basil, chopped
1/4 c. fresh parsley, chopped
salt and pepper to taste

Cook pasta according to package directions; drain. Meanwhile, in a dry skillet over medium-high heat, toast pine nuts for 3 to 5 minutes, until golden. Transfer pine nuts to a bowl. In the same skillet, heat olive oil over medium heat; cook garlic until softened. Remove from heat; stir in lemon zest and juice. In a serving bowl, toss pasta with olive oil mixture, tomatoes, herbs and pine nuts. Season with salt and pepper. Makes 6 servings.

Try flavored pasta in your favorite recipes÷there are so many to choose from! Enjoy pasta flavored with spinach, garlic, basil or even spicy red peppers.

Oodles of Noodles

Crab Fettuccine

Christi Hegstad
Ankeny, IA

This recipe comes from my dear Grandma Farah...aside from being one of the most admirable women I know, she's also a great cook!

8-oz. pkg. fettuccine pasta
2 cloves garlic, minced
1/4 c. butter
1 c. half-and-half
8-oz. can imitation crabmeat

1/8 t. pepper
1/2 c. shredded Parmesan
   cheese
1 c. peas

Prepare pasta according to package directions; drain. In skillet over medium heat, sauté garlic in butter until golden; add half-and-half, crabmeat and pepper. Sauté 3 minutes more; stir occasionally. Mix in Parmesan cheese; heat until melted. Add peas; heat through. Remove from heat; toss with pasta. Serves 4.

Linda's Orzo & Rice

Linda Dominianni
Whitestone, NY

Use in place of rice in stir-fry and seafood recipes.

1 c. orzo, uncooked
1/2 c. butter

2 c. long-cooking rice, uncooked
5 c. water

In a large skillet or saucepan over medium heat, sauté orzo in butter until golden, stirring constantly; add rice. Pour in water slowly; bring to a boil. Cover and simmer over low heat for approximately 20 minutes or until water is absorbed. Remove from heat; let stand a few minutes before serving. Serves 6 to 8.

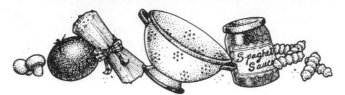

Fruity Chicken Salad

Gail Prather
Bethel, MN

*This is a potluck favorite of mine…I'm always asked
to share the recipe.*

6-oz. pkg. small shell pasta
3 c. chicken, cooked and cubed
2 T. onion, minced
1 t. salt
1-1/2 c. celery, sliced

1-1/2 c. green grapes, halved
1 c. mandarin oranges, drained
1/2 c. slivered almonds, toasted
1 c. mayonnaise
1 c. whipping cream, whipped

Prepare pasta according to package directions; drain and rinse in cold
water. Transfer to a large serving bowl. Add remaining ingredients
except whipped cream; mix well. Cover and refrigerate. Just before
serving fold in whipped cream until well coated; serve chilled. Makes
12 servings.

Try serving Apricot Balls following this fresh
Fruity Chicken Salad! Sweet and just tart enough,
the recipe is on page 200.

Oodles of Noodles

Company Casserole

Gail Harris
Bucyrus, OH

Double or even triple this recipe for an easy meal fit for a crowd.

8-oz. pkg. wide egg noodles
1 onion, chopped
2 T. butter
1-1/2 lbs. ground beef
4-oz. can sliced mushrooms, drained
1/2 c. stuffed olives, sliced
1/2 c. American cheese, diced
1/2 t. salt
1/8 t. pepper
10-3/4 oz. can cream of mushroom soup
1/2 c. milk
1 c. chow mein noodles
4-oz. pkg. chopped cashews

Prepare noodles according to package directions; drain. In a skillet over medium heat, sauté onion in butter until golden. Add beef and cook until no longer pink; drain. Stir in noodles, mushrooms, olives, cheese, salt and pepper; heat through. Pour into an ungreased 2-quart casserole dish. Combine soup and milk; add to dish, stirring well. Bake, uncovered, at 375 degrees for 25 minutes; sprinkle with chow mein noodles and cashews. Return to oven for an additional 15 minutes. Makes 4 to 6 servings.

Need a savory dip that's a hit? Mix a 15-oz. container of cottage cheese with 1/2 package of dry vegetable soup mix and 1/3 cup milk. Combine in a blender until smooth...refrigerate for 30 minutes and serve with crackers and veggies.

Ring Toss Salad

*Pam Heasley
Ree Heights, SD*

Serve alongside grilled chicken breasts or pork chops.

7-oz. pkg. wagon wheel pasta
1 c. mayonnaise
1/2 c. sugar
1/2 T. vinegar

1 head cabbage, shredded
1/2 green pepper, chopped
1 cucumber, chopped
1/4 c. green onions, sliced

Prepare pasta according to package directions; drain and rinse in cold water. In a bowl, combine mayonnaise, sugar and vinegar; mix well and set aside. Add pasta and vegetables to a serving bowl; stir in mayonnaise mixture. Cover; refrigerate until serving. Serves 4 to 6.

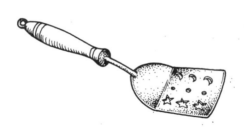

Sausage Fettuccine

*Donna West
Spring Creek, NV*

This recipe has been shared many times with my bowling club.

8-oz. pkg. fettuccine
1 lb. ground pork Italian
    sausage
1 to 2 cloves garlic, chopped
1 onion, chopped

2 T. all-purpose flour
1-1/2 to 2 c. half-and-half
2 to 3 T. grated Parmesan
    cheese
salt and pepper to taste

Prepare pasta according to package directions; drain. In a skillet over medium-high heat, brown sausage, garlic and onion; drain. Whisk in remaining ingredients. Heat thoroughly without boiling. Spoon over fettuccine. Serves 4.

Oodles of **Noodles**

Chicken Club Pasta

Donna Schloemer
Tacoma, WA

Use whatever pasta is in the pantry...rotini, bowtie or penne!

1 lb. bacon, diced
1-1/2 c. half-and-half
2 to 3 T. dried parsley
3/4 c. grated Parmesan cheese
1-lb. pkg. boneless, skinless
    chicken breasts, cooked
    and cubed

Optional: canned sliced
    mushrooms
garlic salt and pepper to taste
12 to 16-oz. pkg. pasta, cooked

In a skillet over medium-high heat, cook bacon until almost crisp; drain. Return to skillet; add half-and-half, parsley, cheese, chicken and mushrooms, if using. Season to taste. Reduce heat; stir and heat for 4 minutes. Spoon over pasta; toss to coat. Makes 6 to 8 servings.

There are many miracles in the world to be celebrated
and, for me, garlic is the most deserving.
–Leo Buscaglia

Tri-Color Pasta Salad

Trina Travis
Jacksonville, TX

Great any time of year but especially yummy in the summertime.

2 yellow squash, diced
2 zucchini, diced
3 roma tomatoes, diced
1/2 c. sweet onion, diced
2 c. broccoli flowerets
3.8-oz. can sliced black olives,
  drained

8-oz. bottle Italian salad
  dressing
16-oz. pkg. tri-color rotini

Combine vegetables in a large serving bowl; pour dressing on top. Cover and refrigerate overnight. Prepare pasta according to package directions; drain and rinse with cold water. Fold into vegetable mixture; gently toss to coat. Makes 8 to 10 servings.

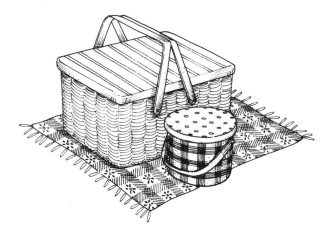

Keep wooden salad bowls looking their best by rubbing them inside and out with wax paper after washing them with warm, soapy water. The wax from the paper will keep the surface of the bowl sealed.

Oodles of Noodles

Tomato-Corn Casserole

Karen Holder
Hamilton, OH

Egg noodles and a sprinkling of cheese will make this a favorite!

16-oz. pkg. medium egg noodles
1 onion, chopped
1 green pepper, chopped
1 T. olive oil
2 lbs. ground beef

14-3/4 oz. can creamed corn
15-oz. can tomato sauce
1 T. cocktail sauce
1 c. shredded Cheddar cheese

Prepare noodles according to package directions; drain. In a skillet, sauté onion and green pepper in olive oil until tender. Add beef; cook until no longer pink. Drain. Stir in noodles and remaining ingredients except cheese; pour into an ungreased 13"x9" baking pan. Bake, uncovered, at 350 degrees for 25 minutes; sprinkle with cheese and return to oven just until cheese melts. Serve warm. Makes 10 to 12 servings.

An easy way to "beef up" any recipe...crumble leftover meatloaf or cut roast beef into bite-size pieces, season to taste and toss into casseroles, soups and sauces.

Mediterranean Spaghetti

Joyce Jongsma
Crete, IL

Light in taste, low in fat and so fast!

6-oz. pkg. spaghetti
1/4 c. golden raisins
1/3 c. warm water
1 T. plus 1 t. olive oil
1/2 c. onion, chopped
2 cloves garlic, minced
12 pitted olives, sliced

1/4 t. red pepper, minced
8-oz. can tuna, drained
1-1/2 c. tomatoes, chopped
    and drained
1 c. tomato sauce
pepper to taste

Prepare spaghetti according to package directions; drain. Add raisins to warm water; set aside. Heat oil in a skillet over low heat; sauté onion and garlic until soft, about 7 to 10 minutes. Add olives and red pepper; increase heat to high. Drain raisins; add to skillet, stirring about 3 to 5 minutes. Stir in tuna, tomatoes and sauce; heat through. Season to taste with pepper. Serve over warm spaghetti. Makes 4 servings.

Add a few extra cloves of garlic to the pan when cooking Mediterranean Spaghetti. After cooking, combine the extra garlic with 1/2 cup of softened butter. Mix well and chill. Spread on thick slices of Italian bread and broil for a few minutes just before serving, until golden and crunchy.

Special-Time Tuna Salad

Kathleen Werner
Laurel, MD

Serve with toasted garlic bread, a green salad or fresh fruit.

16-oz. pkg. rotini
2 c. Catalina salad dressing,
　　divided
1 c. sour cream
2 T. mayonnaise
1 onion, chopped

4 green onions, chopped
1 green pepper, chopped
2 T. fresh chives, chopped
2 to 4 stalks celery, chopped
　　and divided
4 to 6 6-oz. cans tuna, drained

Prepare pasta according to package directions; drain. Combine pasta and 1/2 cup salad dressing; set aside. In a large serving bowl, mix remaining dressing, sour cream and mayonnaise; fold in remaining ingredients. Gently stir in pasta and refrigerate overnight. Makes 10 to 12 servings.

Taking this salad to a picnic? Mix it up in a plastic zipping bag instead of a bowl, seal and set it right in the cooler. No worries about spills or leaks!

Chicken Pasta Salad

Grace Woodruff
Pine Bluff, AR

Serve with toasted pita bread chips.

8-oz. pkg. tri-color pasta
4 boneless, skinless chicken
    breasts, cooked and chopped
11-oz. can mandarin oranges,
    drained
1 sweet onion, chopped
1 green pepper, chopped

3 stalks celery, chopped
8-oz. can water chestnuts,
    drained and chopped
1/2 lb. green grapes, halved
1-1/2 to 2 c. ranch salad
    dressing

Prepare pasta according to package directions; drain and rinse with cold water. In a large bowl, add pasta and remaining ingredients in the order listed. Mix well. Cover and refrigerate before serving. Makes 8 servings.

Tortellini Toss

Nicole Shira
New Baltimore, MI

There are so many varieties of tortellini...try them all!

7-oz. pkg. tortellini pasta
15-1/4 oz. can baby peas,
    drained
minced garlic to taste
1/2 c. olive oil

1 T. lemon juice
1/4 c. white vinegar
fresh grated Parmesan cheese
    to taste

Prepare pasta according to package directions; drain and rinse with cold water. In a large serving bowl, combine pasta and remaining ingredients; toss gently. Cover and chill before serving. Makes 6 to 8 servings.

Oodles of Noodles

Ham & Noodle Skillet

Marcia Clark
Hesperia, MI

Add a can of green beans for a touch of color.

4-oz. can sliced mushrooms
2 c. cooked ham, cubed
1/4 c. onion, chopped
2 T. margarine
1/8 t. pepper
1/8 t. paprika

1 t. Worcestershire sauce
1 c. water
7-oz. pkg. medium egg
    noodles, uncooked
1 c. sour cream

Drain mushrooms; reserve 1/4 cup liquid and set aside. In a skillet over medium heat, sauté ham and onion in margarine; stir in pepper, paprika and Worcestershire sauce. Add water, reserved mushroom liquid and noodles; bring to a boil. Reduce heat and simmer, covered, for 15 minutes. Stir in mushrooms; cook for 5 minutes. Add sour cream; heat through without boiling. Makes 4 servings.

No cooked, cubed ham on hand? Chop up some slices of cooked deli ham to use instead. Deli turkey, chicken and roast beef can all be used in place of cooked meats in recipes...what a time-saver!

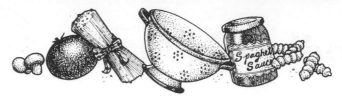

Cheesy Pasta Pie

Marilyn Engelker
Wood River, NE

Sprinkle with shredded mozzarella and make it extra cheesy.

3 c. cooked pasta
2 T. butter, melted
1/2 c. grated Parmesan cheese,
    divided

1-1/4 c. spaghetti sauce
1 t. dried oregano

Combine pasta, butter and 1/4 cup Parmesan cheese; spread in a lightly greased 10" pie plate. Pour spaghetti sauce over top; sprinkle with oregano and remaining Parmesan cheese. Bake, uncovered, at 350 degrees for 30 minutes. Makes 8 servings.

Making homemade spaghetti sauce but don't want to stand over a pot all day? Place the sauce in an oven-safe dish and cook slowly for 2-1/2 hours at 350 degrees for pasta-perfect sauce every time!

Ravioli Casserole

*Donna Nowicki
Center City, MN*

Any stuffed pasta works well…try meat or cheese tortellini too!

28-oz. jar spaghetti sauce,
  divided
25-oz. pkg. frozen cheese
  ravioli, cooked and divided

2 c. cottage cheese, divided
4 c. shredded mozzarella cheese,
  divided
1/4 c. grated Parmesan cheese

Spread 1/2 cup spaghetti sauce in an ungreased 13"x9" baking pan; layer with half the ravioli. Pour 1-1/4 cups sauce over the top; spread one cup cottage cheese and then 2 cups mozzarella cheese over the sauce. Repeat layers; sprinkle with Parmesan cheese. Bake, uncovered, at 350 degrees for 30 to 40 minutes. Let stand 5 to 10 minutes before serving. Serves 6 to 8.

Macaroni & Corn Bake

*Jennifer Steenblock
Des Moines, IA*

Seems like at every family gathering, someone always makes this dish. It's such a hit with kids and adults love it too!

14-3/4 oz. can creamed corn
15-1/4 oz. can corn
1 c. elbow macaroni, uncooked

1/4 c. butter
1 c. pasteurized process cheese
  spread, cubed

Combine ingredients together; pour into a lightly greased 2-quart casserole dish. Bake, covered, at 350 degrees for 45 minutes. Makes 6 to 8 servings.

Noodle Casserole

Jenny Day
Marceline, MO

*I was finally tired of take-out and micro-meals when I decided I was
going to cook something really good. I asked my mother for this recipe
and found that it's really easy and freezes well too!*

8-oz. pkg. fine egg noodles
1 lb. ground beef, browned
15-oz. can tomato sauce
1/2 c. green onions, chopped
1 c. sour cream
1 c. cottage cheese

1 T. margarine, melted
1 t. salt
1/4 t. garlic salt
1/8 t. pepper
1 c. shredded Cheddar cheese

Prepare noodles according to package directions; drain. Combine
noodles and all ingredients except Cheddar cheese; transfer into a
lightly greased 2-quart casserole dish. Sprinkle with Cheddar cheese;
bake, uncovered, at 350 degrees until bubbly, about 30 minutes.
Makes 4 to 6 servings.

Add frozen peas, chopped asparagus or shredded carrots to
this fresh and fast dish...any veggie on hand will work!

Oodles of Noodles

Parmesan Noodles

Laura Carman
Hooper, UT

A side dish to complement chicken, pork or beef.

8-oz. pkg. medium egg noodles, cooked
3 T. green onions, chopped
2 T. butter
1/2 c. grated Parmesan cheese
garlic salt and pepper to taste

Toss ingredients together in a serving bowl; serve warm or cold. Makes 4 to 6 servings.

Mother's Egg Noodles

Gwen Strough
Fortville, IN

Just thought we'd give you an oodle on how to make a noodle.

7 egg yolks
1 egg, beaten
1-1/2 c. all-purpose flour
1/2 t. salt
46-oz. can chicken broth

Blend yolks and egg together until frothy; gradually mix in flour with a fork until a ball forms. Roll dough out thinly on a well-floured surface; cut into 1/4-inch wide strips. Set aside until dry; carefully drop into boiling chicken broth until tender. Serves 8 to 10.

Use Mother's Egg Noodles to whip up homemade chicken noodle soup on a chilly night. Just heat chicken broth, mixed veggies, cooked chicken and these yummy noodles in a big soup kettle…so easy!

Rotini Salad

Lynette Yarbrough
Danville, VA

This colorful salad is good with cooked chicken or tuna mixed in too!

16-oz. pkg. rotini pasta
16-oz. jar slaw dressing
2 15-1/4 oz. cans corn, drained

1 green pepper, diced
2 tomatoes, diced
1 cucumber, peeled and diced

Prepare pasta according to package directions; drain and rinse with cold water. In a serving bowl, combine pasta with remaining ingredients; toss gently. Cover and chill before serving. Makes 8 to 10 servings.

Kraut 'n Shells

Joy Kinnear
Sterling Heights, MI

Also easy to leave in a slow cooker until thoroughly warmed.

14-oz. can sauerkraut, drained
    and rinsed
2 c. small shell pasta, cooked
1-1/2 lbs. Kielbasa sausage,
    thickly sliced

3/4 c. butter, melted
1 T. pepper

Place all ingredients except pepper in a heavy saucepan; mix well. Cook over medium heat until warmed through; stir in pepper before serving. Serves 4.

Life is a combination of magic and pasta.
–Fellini

Oodles of Noodles

Lucky-7 Mac & Cheese

Tina Vogel
Orlando, FL

Wow! This homestyle favorite has seven kinds of cheese!

16-oz. pkg. elbow macaroni
1 c. skim milk
1/2 c. extra-sharp Cheddar
   cheese, cubed
1/2 c. Colby cheese, cubed
1/2 c. pasteurized process
   cheese spread, cubed

1/2 c. Swiss cheese, cubed
1/2 c. provolone cheese, cubed
1/2 c. Monterey Jack cheese,
   cubed
1/2 c. crumbled blue cheese
salt and pepper to taste

Prepare macaroni according to package directions; drain. In a heavy saucepan, combine milk and cheeses. Heat over low to medium heat until melted, stirring often. Mix in macaroni; season with salt and pepper. Heat through. Makes 6 to 8 servings.

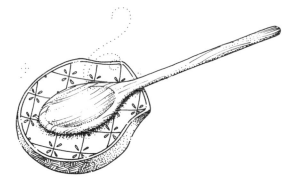

No blue or sharp Cheddar cheese on hand for
Lucky-7 Mac & Cheese? Substitute the family's
favorite cheeses...just make sure there's a
total of 3-1/2 cups of cheese.

Basil-Asparagus Penne

Molly Lamrouex
Owosso, MI

Good hot or cold.

8-oz. pkg. penne pasta
2 T. olive oil
4 cloves garlic, minced
1/8 t. red pepper flakes
1 lb. asparagus, chopped
4 tomatoes, peeled, seeded
 and chopped

1 c. chicken broth
1/3 c. fresh basil, chopped
salt and pepper to taste
2/3 c. grated Parmesan cheese
fresh parsley to taste

Prepare pasta according to package directions; drain. Heat olive oil in a skillet; sauté garlic and red pepper flakes for 2 minutes. Add asparagus, tomatoes, broth and basil; heat, covered, about 8 minutes. Season with salt and pepper. Spoon over pasta; sprinkle with Parmesan cheese and parsley. Makes 4 to 6 servings.

Here's an oh-so-simple pesto recipe to serve with
this pasta dish. Place 2 cloves garlic, 1 cup fresh basil
leaves, 1/3 cup olive oil and salt and pepper to taste in a
food processor and blend until a coarse paste forms.
Combine with butter for a tasty spread.

Seafood Pasta Salad

Mary Lou Thomas
Portland, ME

This is my wonderful sister's recipe...she is an amazing cook! Make early in the day to let the flavors blend. Yummy!

8-oz. pkg. rotini pasta
1/2 c. mayonnaise-type salad
   dressing
1/4 c. Italian salad dressing
2 T. grated Parmesan cheese
1-1/2 c. imitation crabmeat,
   chopped

1 c. frozen broccoli flowerets,
   thawed
1/2 c. green pepper, chopped
1/2 c. tomato, chopped
1/4 c. green onion, sliced

Cook pasta according to package directions; drain and rinse with cold water. In a serving bowl, mix together dressings and Parmesan cheese. Add pasta and remaining ingredients; toss lightly. Cover and refrigerate at least 2 hours. Serves 4 to 6.

Pasta salad is so versatile and works well with just about
any veggies on hand. Toss in chopped celery, cucumbers,
grated carrots or even cheese chunks for
a new dish every time.

Homestyle Mac & Cheese

Karen Crooks
West Des Moines, IA

Serve up this comfort food with a salad on the side!

2 c. cooked macaroni
2 T. butter
2 T. all-purpose flour
3/4 c. milk
1/8 t. salt
pepper to taste
1/2 t. dried, minced onion

1 c. shredded American cheese,
    divided
1 c. shredded Cheddar cheese,
    divided
1 c. sour cream
paprika to taste

Place macaroni in an ungreased 2-quart casserole dish; set aside. Melt butter in a saucepan; whisk in flour, stirring until smooth. Gradually pour in milk; add salt, pepper and onion. Stir in 3/4 cup each American and Cheddar cheeses, stirring until melted. Pour over macaroni. Stir in sour cream until combined. Top with remaining cheeses; sprinkle with paprika. Bake, uncovered, at 350 degrees until golden, about 25 to 30 minutes. Serves 4 to 6.

Blend chocolate milk, a scoop of ice cream and
a spoonful of peanut butter to make a scrumptious
milkshake in minutes.

Turkey Stroganoff

Candi Sparrow
Davie, FL

Make it with ground beef for a hearty twist.

7-oz. pkg. medium egg noodles
3/4 lb. ground turkey
1 T. olive oil
2 beef bouillon cubes, crumbled
1 onion, diced

4-oz. can sliced mushrooms, drained
1 T. margarine
2 cloves garlic, chopped
2 c. sour cream

Prepare noodles according to package directions; drain. In a skillet over medium heat, brown turkey in olive oil. Add bouillon cubes, stirring well. Remove from heat and set aside. In another skillet, sauté onion and mushrooms in margarine; mix in garlic, heating until golden. Combine with turkey mixture. Stir in sour cream. Heat through; do not boil. Arrange warm noodles on serving plates; spoon stroganoff on top. Serves 2 to 4.

Sour cream can be mixed with any of the seasoning blends found at the meat counter. Try some different blends for an endless variety of savory dips!

Zippy Ziti & Broccoli

Jacob Jackson
Phoenix, AZ

A great way to sneak more veggies into dinner.

8-oz. pkg. ziti pasta,
   uncooked
2 c. frozen broccoli cuts
1 clove garlic, minced
16-oz. jar Alfredo sauce
14-1/2 oz. can Italian-style
   diced tomatoes

2 c. shredded mozzarella
   cheese
2 T. Italian-flavored dry
   bread crumbs
2 t. margarine, melted

Prepare ziti according to package directions; add broccoli during last minute of cooking time. Drain; add garlic, Alfredo sauce, tomatoes and cheese, mixing well. Spoon into an ungreased 2-quart casserole dish; set aside. Toss bread crumbs with margarine; sprinkle over ziti. Bake at 350 degrees until top is golden, about 20 to 30 minutes. Makes 4 to 6 servings.

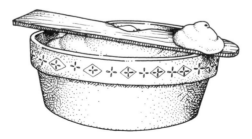

Go Mexican with Zippy Ziti! Combine canned tomato sauce with a jar of salsa for a zesty sauce and use tomatoes with green chiles instead of Italian-style tomatoes. Serve topped with sour cream and chopped green onions.

No-Bake Lasagna

Jennie Gist
Gooseberry Patch

You don't even have to turn on the oven for this lasagna. The noodles and sauce are simply layered on the plate...it's so easy!

4 lasagna noodles, uncooked
1/2 c. sliced mushrooms
1/4 c. onion, chopped
2 t. canola oil
1 c. spaghetti sauce
1/2 c. tomato, chopped

1/4 t. dried basil
1/4 t. pepper
1 c. shredded mozzarella cheese
Garnish: grated Parmesan
    cheese

Cook noodles according to package directions; drain and cut into thirds. Meanwhile, in a skillet over medium heat, cook mushrooms and onion in oil until tender. Stir in spaghetti sauce, tomato, basil and pepper. Bring to a boil. Reduce heat to low; cover and simmer for 10 minutes, stirring occasionally. Add mozzarella cheese; cook until cheese is melted. On a plate, layer 1/4 cup sauce and 4 noodle pieces. Repeat layers 2 more times. Spread with remaining sauce and sprinkle with Parmesan cheese. Makes 2 servings.

Beans add flavor to hearty recipes...try mashed cannellini, kidney, black or pinto beans in place of, or in addition to, ground beef.

Peas & Pasta Shells

Kendall Hale
Lynn, MA

This is a delicious meat-free alternative for when you need dinner in a snap!

2 c. small pasta shells, uncooked
1/4 c. olive oil
1/4 c. butter
1 c. onion, finely chopped
2 cloves garlic, minced

2-1/2 c. frozen peas
1/4 c. fresh parsley, finely
   chopped
1/2 t. salt
pepper to taste

Cook pasta according to package directions; drain. Meanwhile, in a skillet, heat olive oil and butter. Sauté onion and garlic until tender. Add pasta, peas, parsley, salt and pepper; mix well. Transfer to an ungreased 13"x9" baking pan. Cover and bake at 350 degrees for 15 minutes, or until heated through. Makes 6 servings.

Garlic-Angel Hair Pasta

Terry Esposito
Freehold, NJ

Tastes great with broccoli or carrots on the side.

16-oz. pkg. angel hair pasta
7 cloves garlic, minced

1/3 c. olive oil
1-1/3 c. seasoned bread crumbs

Prepare pasta according to package directions; drain. In a skillet over low heat, sauté garlic in olive oil until golden. Pour garlic and oil over pasta; sprinkle with bread crumbs. Mix well; cover and let stand for 2 minutes before serving. Makes 8 servings.

When roasting garlic, roast a whole head instead of individual cloves. Any extra can be squeezed out into a plastic zipping bag and frozen. Roasted garlic is so handy for sauces, spreads and to add punch to ready-made salad dressings.

Oodles of Noodles

Pizza Pasta Salad

Julia List
Lincoln, NE

This salad has such a wonderful tangy flavor and it's always a hit at potlucks and cookouts. It complements any meal and there are rarely any leftovers...be sure to help yourself first!

16-oz. pkg. tri-color rotini
2 tomatoes, seeded and diced
6-oz. can black olives, drained
1 sweet onion, sliced
1/2 lb. Cheddar cheese, cubed
1/2 lb. mozzarella cheese, cubed
3-oz. pkg. sliced pepperoni
3/4 c. oil

3/4 c. grated Parmesan cheese
1/2 c. red wine vinegar
2 t. dried oregano
1 t. garlic powder
1 t. salt
1/4 t. pepper
cayenne pepper to taste

Prepare pasta according to package directions; drain and rinse with cold water. In a large serving bowl, mix pasta, vegetables, Cheddar and mozzarella cheeses and pepperoni; set aside. In a separate bowl, whisk remaining ingredients together; pour over pasta mixture. Stir; cover and refrigerate until serving. Serves 16.

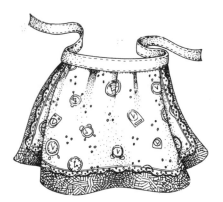

Even easier...instead of whipping up the salad dressing in this recipe, use ready-made Italian salad dressing instead.

Thai Peanut Noodles

*Emily Selmer
Sumner, WA*

Not a shrimp lover? Substitute chicken breasts instead.

1 lb. shrimp, cleaned and cooked
1 c. light Italian salad dressing, divided
8-oz. pkg. angel hair pasta
2 T. crunchy peanut butter
1 T. soy sauce
1 T. honey
1 t. ground ginger
1/2 t. red pepper flakes
1 carrot, peeled and shredded
1 c. green onions, chopped
1 T. sesame oil
2 T. fresh cilantro, chopped
Optional: 2/3 c. chopped peanuts

Coat shrimp with 1/2 cup salad dressing; refrigerate for 30 minutes. Meanwhile, prepare pasta according to package directions; drain. In a bowl, whisk peanut butter with remaining salad dressing, soy sauce, honey, ginger and red pepper flakes until smooth; set aside. In a skillet over medium heat, sauté carrot, onions and shrimp in sesame oil until shrimp is cooked, about 5 minutes. Toss pasta, peanut butter mixture and shrimp together in a large serving bowl; sprinkle with cilantro and peanuts, if desired. Serves 4.

Need to chop nuts in a hurry? Place them in a plastic zipping bag and roll with a rolling pin...so easy!

Asparagus & Pine Nuts

Andrea Vernon
Logansport, IN

Sometimes we make this dish with ravioli or bowtie pasta...a yummy variation!

7-oz. pkg. tortellini pasta
3 T. onion, minced
3 cloves garlic, minced
3 T. fresh basil, chopped
1/3 c. butter, melted
2-1/2 c. plum tomatoes, chopped
1 lb. asparagus, trimmed,
   steamed and chopped

1/2 c. pine nuts, toasted
salt and Italian seasoning
   to taste
1/2 c. whipping cream
1/2 c. grated Parmesan cheese

Prepare pasta according to package directions; drain. In a skillet, sauté onion, garlic and basil in butter; stir in tomatoes, asparagus, pine nuts, salt and Italian seasoning. Bring to a boil. Reduce heat; mix in cream, stirring constantly until thickened. Spoon over pasta; sprinkle with Parmesan cheese. Serve warm. Makes 4 to 6 servings.

The easiest way to steam asparagus is to trim the ends
of each stalk, toss into a skillet with about 1/2 inch
of water and cover. When the asparagus
turn bright green, they're ready!

Nutty Chicken Spaghetti

Margo Belkofer
Colorado Springs, CO

Almonds add crunch to this creamy dish.

16-oz. pkg. spaghetti
10-3/4 oz. can cream of
  chicken soup
10-3/4 oz. can cream of
  mushroom soup
3/4 c. half-and-half
1/2 c. shredded Cheddar cheese
1/2 c. slivered almonds
1 pimento, sliced thinly
2 c. chicken, cooked and
  chopped
paprika to taste

Prepare pasta according to package directions; drain. Heat soups, half-and-half and cheese in a heavy saucepan over medium heat until cheese melts; do not boil. Remove from heat; add pasta, almonds and pimento. Fold in chicken and spread in an ungreased 2-quart casserole dish; sprinkle with paprika. Bake, uncovered, at 325 degrees for 20 minutes, or until heated through. Makes 6 to 8 servings.

Keep a pair of scissors in the kitchen to make quick work of dicing tomatoes, shredding lettuce, chopping celery and even cutting up chicken for casseroles!

Pork & Bean Spaghetti

Marilyn Golema
Wyandotte, MI

A family favorite.

16-oz. pkg. spaghetti
1 onion, chopped
2 T. olive oil
16-oz. can pork & beans
1 T. sugar

14-1/2 oz. can diced tomatoes
10-oz. pkg. frozen broccoli
  flowerets
Garnish: grated Parmesan
  cheese

Prepare spaghetti according to package directions; drain. Meanwhile, in a skillet over medium heat, sauté onion in olive oil until tender. Add pork & beans, sugar and tomatoes. Bring to a boil; reduce heat and simmer for 10 minutes. Stir in broccoli; simmer another 15 to 20 minutes. Add spaghetti; gently stir until well combined. Let stand for 15 minutes before serving; sprinkle with Parmesan cheese. Makes 8 servings.

Need to cool dinner down quickly to freeze for later?
Divide it into individual servings first and refrigerate.
Freezing single-size entrées makes dinner
a breeze...just thaw and reheat!

Sour Cream-Beef Casserole

Mary Burns
Hurricane, WV

This recipe was passed to me many years ago...it's a family favorite.

12-oz. pkg. wide egg noodles
1 lb. ground beef
29-oz. can tomato sauce
1/2 t. salt
1/8 t. pepper
1/8 t. dried oregano

1 c. sour cream
2/3 c. cream cheese, softened
1/2 onion, finely chopped
1/2 green pepper, minced
2 c. shredded mozzarella cheese, divided

Prepare noodles according to package directions; drain and set aside. Meanwhile, brown beef in a skillet over medium heat; drain. Stir in tomato sauce and seasonings. Combine noodles with sour cream, cream cheese, onion and green pepper; mix well. Spread half the noodle mixture in an ungreased 13"x9" baking pan. Layer half the beef mixture over top; sprinkle with half the mozzarella cheese. Repeat layers. Bake, uncovered, at 350 degrees for 20 to 25 minutes, until hot and bubbly. Makes 12 servings.

Need a snack to tide the family over until dinner? Head to the pantry and mix up cereal, raisins, chocolate chips, coconut and mixed nuts in a big bowl. Scoop into individual bowls or cups and let them enjoy!

Hearty in a Hurry

Anytime Stuffed Peppers

Kelly Marcum
Dixon, IL

Make the filling ahead of time for a speedy dinner!

1 lb. ground beef
2 15-oz. cans tomato sauce
2-1/4 oz. can sliced black
　olives, drained
4-oz. can sliced mushrooms,
　drained
1 t. Italian seasoning

1/2 t. garlic powder
1 t. fresh parsley, chopped
1 to 1-1/2 c. instant rice,
　uncooked
hot pepper sauce to taste
3 green peppers, halved
2 c. shredded mozzarella cheese

In a skillet over medium heat, brown beef; drain. Stir in remaining ingredients except green peppers and cheese. Spoon beef mixture into peppers; arrange in an ungreased 13"x9" baking pan. Cover and bake at 375 degrees until peppers are tender, about 35 to 45 minutes. Sprinkle with cheese; bake, uncovered, an additional 5 minutes or until cheese melts. Makes 6 servings.

Super speedy stuffed peppers! Just fill with leftover spaghetti or other pasta in sauce, top with shredded cheese and bake until golden and bubbly.

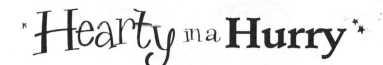# Hearty in a Hurry

Muffin-Tin Pizza Loaves

Shelley Turner
Boise, ID

A delicious twist on meatloaf that your whole family will love!

1 egg, beaten
1/2 c. pizza sauce
1/4 c. seasoned dry bread
   crumbs
1/2 t. Italian seasoning

1-1/2 lbs. ground beef
1-1/2 c. shredded mozzarella
   cheese
Optional: additional pizza sauce,
   warmed

In a large bowl, combine egg, pizza sauce, bread crumbs and Italian seasoning. Crumble beef over mixture and mix well. Divide among 12 greased muffin cups; press onto the bottom and up the sides. Fill centers with cheese. Bake, uncovered, at 375 degrees for 15 to 18 minutes, or until meat is no longer pink. Serve immediately with pizza sauce, if desired. Makes 12 servings.

Easy Mini Meatloaves

Jen Licon-Conner
Gooseberry Patch

All the goodness of meatloaf in a fraction of the time!

12-oz. tube refrigerated biscuits
1-1/2 lbs. ground beef
1 c. catsup, divided
1/2 c. onion, chopped

1 egg, beaten
1/4 c. quick-cooking oats,
   uncooked
1 c. shredded Cheddar cheese

Divide and press biscuit dough into the bottom and up the sides of 10 greased muffin cups; set aside. In a bowl, combine beef, 1/2 cup catsup, onion, egg and oats; mix well. Form beef mixture into 10 balls; place one in each muffin cup. Spread remaining catsup over top; sprinkle with cheese. Bake, uncovered, at 350 degrees for 30 minutes, or until cooked through. Makes 10 servings.

Pork Schnitzel

Irene Robinson
Cincinnati, OH

Serve with fresh green beans, applesauce and hot, buttery rolls.

6 1/2-inch thick boneless
   pork chops
1/2 t. salt
1/3 c. all-purpose flour

1/4 c. bread crumbs
1 egg, beaten
1/4 c. milk
3 T. oil

Place pork chops between wax paper and pound to 1/8-inch thickness; season both sides with salt. Combine flour and bread crumbs; set aside. Whisk egg and milk together in a pie plate; set aside. Dip pork chops into egg mixture; coat with flour mixture. In a skillet over medium-high heat, brown both sides of pork chops in oil, about 3 minutes per side, or until cooked through. Makes 6 servings.

Need a quick dessert? Peel, core and halve two Granny Smith apples. Place in microwave-safe bowls, add a few tablespoons of water and sprinkle with cinnamon-sugar. Microwave on high for a minute or two, until tender. Yum!

Caramel Apple Pork Chops

Nola Coons
Gooseberry Patch

These yummy pork chops will impress your guests!

2 t. oil
4 boneless pork chops
2 T. brown sugar, packed
1/8 t. cinnamon
1/8 t. nutmeg

salt and pepper to taste
2 T. butter
2 Granny Smith apples, cored,
   peeled and sliced
Garnish: 3 T. chopped pecans

Heat oil in a skillet over medium-high heat. Cook chops for 5 to 6 minutes on each side, until browned and fully cooked. Remove to a serving platter; keep warm. In a small bowl, combine brown sugar, cinnamon, nutmeg, salt and pepper. Add butter to skillet; stir in apples and brown sugar mixture. Cover and cook for 3 to 4 minutes, until apples are tender. Use a slotted spoon to transfer apples to the serving platter; keep warm. Continue cooking mixture in skillet, uncovered, until sauce thickens slightly. Spoon sauce over apples and chops; garnish with pecans. Makes 4 servings.

Only using half an onion? Rub the remaining side
with butter or olive oil and store in the fridge in
a plastic zipping bag. It will stay fresh for weeks.

Zesty Pizza Casserole

Valerie Neeley
Robinson, IL

Add your favorite pizza toppings to this easy casserole.

1 lb. ground beef
1/2 c. onion, chopped
1/2 c. green pepper, chopped
2 c. cooked elbow macaroni
2 15-oz. cans pizza sauce
4-oz. can sliced mushrooms,
  drained
4-oz. pkg. sliced pepperoni

1/2 t. dried oregano
1/2 t. garlic powder
1/2 t. dried basil
1/2 t. salt
3/4 c. shredded mozzarella
  cheese
Garnish: sliced fresh basil

Brown beef with onion and green pepper in a large skillet over medium heat. Drain; stir in remaining ingredients except cheese and garnish. Transfer to a lightly greased 2-quart casserole dish; sprinkle with cheese. Bake, uncovered, at 350 degrees for 30 to 45 minutes, until hot and bubbly. Garnish with basil.. Makes 4 to 6 servings.

Make brown & serve dinner rolls extra yummy! Before baking, brush with a little beaten egg and sprinkle with Parmesan cheese and Italian seasoning.

Easy Stromboli

Jane Evans
De Graff, OH

Serve with warmed garlic butter or pizza sauce for dipping.

1 loaf frozen bread dough,
   thawed
2 eggs, separated
2 T. oil
1 t. dried oregano
1 t. dried parsley

1/2 t. garlic powder
1/4 t. pepper
4-oz. pkg. sliced pepperoni
8-oz. pkg. shredded mozzarella
   cheese
1 T. grated Parmesan cheese

On a lightly floured surface, roll out dough into a 15-inch by 12-inch rectangle. Combine egg yolks, oil and seasonings; spread over dough. Arrange pepperoni and mozzarella cheese over dough; sprinkle with Parmesan cheese. Starting at one long side, roll up; pinch ends to seal. Place seam-side down on a lightly greased baking sheet. Brush with beaten egg whites. Bake at 350 degrees for 30 to 40 minutes, until golden. Slice; serve warm. Makes 8 servings.

No prepared spaghetti sauce on hand? Try this simple, fresh tomato sauce instead...adjust the veggies to taste and according to how much pasta you're making. Sauté chopped onion and garlic in olive oil until softened. Add chopped tomatoes and simmer ten minutes. Season with fresh herbs just before serving. So simple!

Meatball Sub Casserole

Christi Wroe
Bedford, PA

*Serve this tasty casserole with a green salad and
garlic bread...delicious!*

1 loaf Italian bread, cut into
   1-inch thick slices
8-oz. pkg. cream cheese,
   softened
1/2 c. mayonnaise
1 t. Italian seasoning
1/4 t. pepper

2 c. shredded mozzarella cheese,
   divided
1-lb. pkg. frozen meatballs,
   thawed
28-oz. jar pasta sauce
1 c. water

Arrange bread slices in a single layer in an ungreased 13"x9" baking
pan; set aside. In a bowl, combine cream cheese, mayonnaise and
seasonings; spread over bread slices. Sprinkle with 1/2 cup cheese;
set aside. Gently mix together meatballs, spaghetti sauce and water;
spoon over cheese. Sprinkle with remaining cheese. Bake, uncovered,
at 350 degrees for 30 minutes. Serves 4.

Making meatballs from scratch? Instead of baking,
cook 'em quick by just dropping into boiling water.
They'll be lower in fat and will keep their shape too! Boil
for a few minutes and they'll be ready to go into
sauces or into the freezer for another day.

Hearty in a Hurry

Mexican Shepherd's Pie

Vickie
Gooseberry Patch

Round up the family for a pie full of flavor...ready in 30 minutes!

7-oz. pkg. 4-cheese instant
   mashed potato flakes
1 lb. lean ground beef
1/2 c. green onions, sliced and
   divided
1 c. barbecue sauce
4-oz. can chopped green chiles

11-oz. can sweet corn & diced
   peppers, drained and divided
1-1/2 c. hot water
1/3 c. milk
2 T. butter
1/2 c. shredded Cheddar cheese
1 c. corn chips

Set aside one pouch of instant mashed potato flakes for future use.
Cook beef and half the onions in a skillet over medium high heat,
stirring occasionally, until beef is browned; drain. Stir in barbecue
sauce, chiles and 3/4 cup corn & diced peppers. Heat to boiling; reduce
heat to low. Meanwhile, prepare one pouch instant mashed potato
flakes according to package directions, using hot water, milk and
butter. Stir in remaining onions and corn & diced peppers; let stand
5 minutes. Spoon potatoes over beef mixture; sprinkle with cheese.
Cover, remove from heat and let stand 5 minutes, or until cheese is
melted. Sprinkle with corn chips. Makes 6 servings.

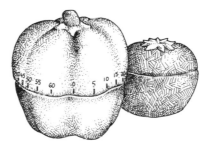

Want a twist on a traditional casserole? Try this tasty
topper...combine frozen shredded hashbrowns with a can
of cream of celery or mushroom soup and spread on top.
Add any favorite seasonings and really spice it up!

Pork Chop Casserole

Kimberly Sawyer
Moyock, NC

Substitute any veggie for the peas for variety.

4 to 6 pork chops
2 T. oil
5 to 6 potatoes, peeled, cubed
  and boiled
10-3/4 oz. can cream of
  mushroom soup
10-3/4 oz. can cream of
  celery soup
15-1/4 oz. can peas
1/2 c. milk
salt and pepper to taste
paprika to taste

In a skillet over medium heat, brown pork chops in oil on both sides; transfer to an ungreased 13"x9" baking pan. Layer potatoes over pork chops; set aside. In a bowl, mix soups, peas and milk; spread over potatoes. Sprinkle with paprika. Bake, uncovered, at 350 degrees for 35 to 40 minutes. Serves 4 to 6.

Mom's Pork Chop Pie

Debbie Rieder
Staunton, VA

Serve this savory supper with mixed veggies.

1 onion, chopped
1 T. butter
2 redskin potatoes, quartered
4 pork chops
1/4 c. water
2/3 c. milk
2-1/4 c. biscuit baking mix

In a skillet over medium heat, sauté onion in butter until tender; place in a greased 4-quart casserole dish. Arrange potatoes on top. In the same skillet, brown pork chops. Remove pork chops; pour water into skillet and whisk into drippings. Drizzle over potatoes; arrange pork chops on top. In a bowl, combine milk and biscuit mix. Roll dough out to cover baking pan; arrange over pork chops. Bake, uncovered, at 350 degrees for 15 to 20 minutes or until golden. Serves 4.

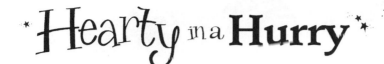

Hearty in a Hurry

Autumn Pork Chops

Michelle McCauley
Garland, TX

Add a baked sweet potato and tall glass of cider
to welcome autumn!

4 pork chops	3 T. brown sugar, packed
4 T. butter, divided	2 t. cinnamon
2 red apples, cored and halved	

Arrange pork chops in an ungreased 13"x9" baking pan; spread one tablespoon butter over each pork chop. Lay one apple half cut-side down on each pork chop; sprinkle with brown sugar and cinnamon. Bake, uncovered, at 350 degrees for 30 to 45 minutes or until pork chop centers are no longer pink. Makes 4 servings.

Pork chops for dinner? Sprinkle a little salt in the
frying pan before browning for less spattering
and more flavorful chops.

Ham & Pineapple Kabobs

Stephanie Moon
Nampa, ID

Soak wooden kabob skewers in water at least 20 minutes before using...they won't burn or stick.

2 lbs. smoked ham, cut into
   1-inch cubes
2 8-oz. cans pineapple chunks,
   drained and juice reserved

8 to 10 skewers, soaked in water
1/4 c. soy sauce
1/4 c. brown sugar, packed
1/4 t. ground ginger

Thread ham cubes and pineapple chunks on skewers; place in an ungreased 2-quart casserole dish. Combine reserved juice and remaining ingredients; pour over kabobs, turning to coat. Cover and refrigerate for 2 hours, turning occasionally. Grill over medium-hot coals, turning twice and brushing with marinade until hot and golden, about 10 minutes. Makes 8 to 10 servings.

After this sweet and savory dinner, surprise the family with a dose of sunshine! Try the recipe for Slice of Sunshine Cake on page 209 for a tropical treat.

Skillet Ham & Cheese

Kathy Hutchings
Lebanon, PA

This creamy recipe is always a favorite.

1/4 c. onion, chopped	3-1/2 c. milk
1/3 c. green pepper, chopped	2 c. cooked ham, cubed
1/4 c. butter, melted	8-oz. pkg. elbow macaroni
1 T. all-purpose flour	1 c. sour cream
1 t. salt	1 c. shredded Swiss cheese

In a skillet over medium heat, sauté onion and green pepper in butter until tender; stir in flour and salt. Gradually whisk in milk; add ham and uncooked macaroni. Bring mixture to a boil, stirring constantly; reduce heat and simmer for 15 minutes, or until macaroni is tender. Stir in sour cream and cheese until cheese melts; do not boil. Makes 6 servings.

Cheese always makes dinner more tasty! Split
brown & serve dinner rolls partly in half and sprinkle
Cheddar or Swiss cheese and chopped green onion or
parsley inside. Bake until golden.

American Tacos

Becky Newkirk
Ashland, MO

Serve in either crunchy or soft taco shells...olé!

2 lbs. ground beef
8-oz. can creamed corn
8-oz. can tomato sauce
1/3 c. cornmeal
2-1/4 oz. can sliced black olives,
    drained

1 c. milk
1 t. chili powder
10 to 12 taco shells

In a skillet over medium-high heat, brown beef until no longer pink; drain. Add remaining ingredients except taco shells; mix well. Spread into an ungreased 2-quart casserole dish. Bake, uncovered, at 350 degrees for 30 minutes. Spoon into taco shells. Makes 10 to 12 servings.

Crunchy Ranch Casserole

Sandie Martens
Fairview, OK

We love this casserole topped with sour cream, black olives and chopped green onion.

1 lb. ground beef
1 onion, diced
15-oz. can ranch-style beans
10-3/4 oz. can cream of
    mushroom soup

3 c. tortilla chips, crushed
1 c. shredded Cheddar cheese

Brown beef and onion in a skillet over medium heat; drain. Stir in beans, soup and chips. Pour into a greased 13"x9" baking pan; bake, uncovered, at 350 degrees for 15 to 20 minutes. Sprinkle with cheese; return to oven until cheese melts. Let stand for 10 minutes before serving. Serves 6.

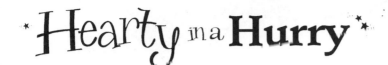

Tangy Taco Ring

Kim Gludt
Anaheim, CA

Makes a fun presentation as well as a delicious dinner!

1/2 lb. ground beef, browned
1-1/4 oz. pkg. taco seasoning
   mix
1 c. shredded Cheddar cheese
2 T. water

2 8-oz. tubes refrigerated
   crescent rolls
1 c. salsa
Optional: sour cream

Combine beef, seasoning mix, cheese and water in a bowl; set aside. Divide crescent rolls into triangles; arrange in a circle on a baking sheet with bases overlapping and ends pointing toward the outside. Shift and flatten dough until there is a solid 5-inch circle of dough in the center with points extending outward. Spoon beef mixture into center of rolls; fold points of triangles up over the filling and toward the center, pinching dough together where the points meet. Filling will not be completely covered. Bake, uncovered, at 350 degrees until golden, about 20 to 25 minutes. Spoon salsa over the top; serve with a dollop of sour cream, if desired. Makes 8 servings.

Look for festive sombreros at party supply stores...
line with brightly colored cloth napkins and serve up
tortilla chips in style!

Pork & Pears

Theresa Jakab
Milford, CT

Pears and balsamic vinegar give this dish its kick.

3 T. butter, divided
2 pears, cored and thinly sliced
1 t. brown sugar, packed
4 1-inch thick pork chops

1 T. all-purpose flour
1 c. chicken broth
1 T. balsamic vinegar

Melt one tablespoon butter in a skillet over medium heat; add pears and brown sugar. Stir occasionally until tender, about 5 to 10 minutes; transfer to a bowl and set aside. In the same skillet, melt remaining butter; brown pork chops on both sides until cooked through. Remove pork chops to a platter; keep warm. Stir flour into drippings; gradually whisk in broth and vinegar until thick and bubbly. Return pork chops to skillet; warm through. Serve pears over pork chops. Makes 4 servings.

Keep a spray mister full of lime or lemon juice in the fridge. So handy for spritzing sliced pears, apples or peaches... prevents browning and adds an extra zing too!

Hearty in a **Hurry**

Pork Tenderloin with Roasted Grapes

Tiffany Brinkley
Broomfield, CO

Your guests will be wowed by this dish...they'll never guess it was so easy to prepare.

1 t. fennel seed, crushed
1/2 t. salt
1/2 t. pepper
1-lb. pork tenderloin

2 t. olive oil
1-1/2 c. seedless red grapes
1-1/2 c. seedless green grapes
1/2 c. chicken broth

In a bowl, stir together fennel seed, salt and pepper. Rub mixture over tenderloin; set aside. In an oven-proof skillet, cook tenderloin in oil 5 minutes, turning to brown all sides. Add grapes and broth to skillet; heat to boiling. Cover and bake at 475 degrees until fully cooked, about 15 to 18 minutes. Transfer pork to a platter and keep warm. Return skillet with grape mixture to stovetop; bring to a boil over high heat. Cook and stir until liquid has thickened, about one minute. Slice pork; serve with grapes and sauce from the skillet. Serves 4.

A quick and tasty appetizer in a jiffy...place a block of cream cheese on a pretty plate, spoon sweet-hot pepper jelly over it and serve with crunchy crackers.

Zesty Mexican Bake

Robyn Oleson Fiedler
Tacoma, WA

Makes a yummy filling for burritos, too!

1 lb. ground beef
2 to 3 cloves garlic, minced
11-1/2 oz. can bean with
    bacon soup
8-oz. can picante sauce, divided
1 t. dried parsley
1 t. paprika
1 t. salt
1/4 t. pepper
16-oz. can kidney beans,
    drained and rinsed

15-oz. can black beans, drained
    and rinsed
1-1/4 c. shredded Cheddar
    cheese, divided
1/2 c. green onions, sliced and
    divided
2/3 c. potato chips, crushed
Garnish: sour cream, olives,
    additional picante sauce,
    shredded cheese, chopped
    green onions

In a skillet, brown beef with garlic; drain and set aside. In a large
bowl, combine soup, picante sauce and seasonings; mix well. Fold in
beans, cheese, onions and beef mixture; spread into an ungreased
2-quart casserole dish. Sprinkle with potato chips. Bake, uncovered, at
425 degrees for 30 to 35 minutes; let stand 5 minutes before serving.
Garnish with sour cream, olives, picante sauce, cheese and onions.
Serves 4.

Have a fiesta! After this
south-of-the-border dinner,
serve up some Mexican "fried"
ice cream. Freeze individual
scoops of ice cream while
dinner's cooking, roll in crushed
frosted corn flake cereal and
drizzle with honey. Top with
a sprinkle of cinnamon,
whipped cream and a cherry!

Hearty in a Hurry

Pepper Steak

Zoe Groff
Saybrook, IL

This hearty dish is sure to be a hit at any party...and they'll never know it only took you 10 minutes to put it together!

1 to 1-1/2 lbs. beef round steak,
   cut into bite-size pieces
1/3 c. all-purpose fl our
1/4 t. pepper
1 onion, sliced
1 green and/or red pepper, sliced

14-1/2 oz. can diced tomatoes
4-oz. can sliced mushrooms,
   drained
3 T. soy sauce
cooked rice

Place roast in a slow cooker. Sprinkle with fl our and pepper; stir well to coat meat. Add remaining ingredients except rice. Cover and cook on high setting for one hour; reduce to low setting and cook for an additional 8 hours. Serve over cooked rice. Makes 4 to 6 servings.

Making rice for dinner? Make some extra and freeze one-cup servings in plastic zipping bags. Add veggies and warm in the microwave for a quick lunch.

Cheesy Beef Casserole

Lori Graham
Lancaster, PA

Homemade milkshakes go hand-in-hand with this hearty dish.

1/2 lb. ground beef
1/4 c. onion, chopped
1/4 c. celery, chopped
1 t. salt
1/8 t. pepper
4 c. bread, cubed

3 T. butter, melted
2 eggs, beaten
1 c. milk
1 c. shredded sharp Cheddar
   cheese

In a skillet over medium heat, brown beef with onion, celery, salt and pepper; drain. Combine with remaining ingredients; spread in a greased 2-quart casserole dish. Bake, uncovered, at 350 degrees for 35 minutes; let stand 5 minutes before serving. Serves 4.

Looking for a lighter milkshake? Combine 1/2 cup flavored yogurt with 1/2 cup fruit juice and a handful of fresh fruit. Whip up in the blender and enjoy!

Cheeseburger Pie

Julie Bedwell
Bainbridge, IN

Served outside on the picnic table, this is a lunch the kids will love!

1 lb. ground beef
10-3/4 oz. can cream of
   mushroom soup

2-lb. pkg. frozen potato puffs
8-oz. pkg. shredded Cheddar
   cheese, divided

In a skillet over medium heat, brown beef; drain. Stir in soup; set aside. Arrange potato puffs over the bottom and up the sides of an ungreased 1-1/2 quart casserole dish, reserving any remaining for use in another recipe. Fill with half the beef mixture; sprinkle with half the cheese. Repeat layers. Bake, uncovered, at 350 degrees until potato puffs are golden, about 20 minutes. Serves 4.

dinner
at
6 pm
tonight!

Grilling out? Burgers don't have to be ordinary...try making them with ground turkey, chicken or even ground sausage. Season them with seasoning blends found at the meat counter. Try Italian, Mexican, Thai, Southwest or Mediterranean!

Skillet Enchiladas

Julie Coles
Boise, ID

Try diced potatoes in place of ground beef
for a vegetarian twist.

1/4 c. oil
8 8-inch corn tortillas
3 c. shredded Cheddar cheese,
 divided

1/2 c. olives, chopped

Heat oil in a skillet; add one tortilla, heating until just softened. Remove to paper towel; pat dry. Repeat with remaining tortillas. Fill tortillas evenly using 2-1/2 cups cheese and olives; roll up and place seam-side down in an electric skillet over medium heat. Pour Enchilada Sauce over the top; heat, covered, for 5 minutes. Sprinkle with remaining cheese; heat, uncovered, until melted. Makes 8.

Enchilada Sauce:

1 lb. ground beef
1/2 c. onion, chopped
2 T. chopped green chiles
1/3 c. milk

10-3/4 oz. can cream of
 mushroom soup
10-oz. can enchilada sauce

In a skillet over medium heat, brown beef with onion; drain. Stir in remaining ingredients; simmer for 20 to 25 minutes.

Enchilada casserole! Instead of rolling tortillas up enchilada style, just cut into strips, layer filling and sauce and bake until heated through.

Hearty in a Hurry

Chili-Cornbread Round

Sharon Miller
Dallas, TX

The cornbread crust is so yummy!

1 lb. ground beef
15-1/2 oz. can red kidney beans
10-1/2 oz. can Italian tomato
    soup
2 to 4 T. chili powder
1/2 t. cumin
1/4 t. nutmeg

1/2 t. hot pepper sauce
11-1/2 oz. tube refrigerated
    cornbread twists
1 c. sour cream
2 T. all-purpose flour
1 c. shredded Cheddar cheese

In a large skillet over medium heat, brown beef; drain. Add beans, soup, seasonings and hot sauce; bring to a boil. Reduce heat; simmer, uncovered, for 5 minutes, stirring often. Separate corn twists into coils. Arrange in a lightly greased 10" pie plate; press to cover the bottom and extend dough 1/2 inch above the rim. Spoon beef mixture into pie plate; set aside. Mix sour cream and flour together; spread over top. Sprinkle with cheese; place pie plate on a baking sheet. Bake, uncovered, at 375 degrees for 30 minutes; let stand 10 minutes before serving. Makes 8 servings.

Chili and cornbread is one combination that can't be beat and leftover chili can make a quick and hearty casserole. Start with about 4 cups of chili, add a can of corn and spoon cornbread batter over everything. Top with a sprinkle of shredded cheese and bake for a filling (and tasty!) dinner.

Ham & Potato Casserole

Sally Jukola
Manitou Springs, CO

Instant mashed potatoes make this recipe even quicker!

1/3 c. green pepper, chopped
2 T. onion, chopped
2 T. butter
10-3/4 oz. can cream of
    mushroom soup

1/2 c. milk
2 t. mustard
1/2 t. pepper
3 c. cooked ham, cubed
2 c. prepared mashed potatoes

In a skillet over medium heat, sauté green pepper and onion in butter until tender; add remaining ingredients except mashed potatoes. Bring to a boil; remove from heat and pour into an ungreased 2-quart casserole dish. Arrange mashed potatoes in a ring on top. Bake, uncovered, at 350 degrees for 20 minutes. Serves 4.

The potato, like man, was not meant to dwell alone.
–Sheila Hibben

Hearty in a Hurry

Brown Sugar Ham Roll-Ups
Lisa Colombo
Appleton, WI

I remember this easy dish from my childhood…Grandma made it for special dinners at her house.

12-oz. pkg. spaghetti
4 t. mustard
6 T. brown sugar, packed
10 slices cooked ham

3 T. onion, minced
3 T. green pepper, minced
2-1/2 c. tomatoes, chopped
3 T. fresh parsley, minced

Prepare spaghetti according to package directions; drain and rinse in cold water. In a small bowl, combine mustard and brown sugar; spread over ham slices. Sprinkle onion and green pepper evenly over ham slices; lay some spaghetti lengthwise down the center of each ham slice. Roll up ham; secure with a toothpick. Place in an ungreased 2-quart casserole dish; layer tomatoes on top. Bake, uncovered, at 350 degrees for 25 minutes; sprinkle with parsley before serving. Makes 10 servings.

Make a crunchy, fresh salad fast with fewer dishes to wash! Toss lettuce, veggies and any other toppers all in a one-gallon plastic zipping bag. Give it a shake and pour into salad bowls.

Beef Stroganoff

Elizabeth Watters
Edwardsville, IL

Spoon over a heap of homestyle egg noodles.

1/4 c. all-purpose flour
1/2 t. salt
1 t. paprika
1/4 t. pepper
1-lb. boneless sirloin steak,
    cubed

1/4 c. butter
2 cloves garlic, minced
1 c. beef broth
1/2 c. water
2 c. sliced mushrooms
1/2 c. sour cream

Combine flour, salt, paprika and pepper in a plastic zipping bag; add steak, shaking to coat. Melt butter in a skillet over medium heat; brown steak with garlic. Add broth, water and mushrooms; mix well. Bring to a boil; reduce heat and simmer, covered, until steak is tender, about 30 minutes. Stir in sour cream; heat thorough but do not boil. Serves 4.

Hot Beef Gravy

Judy Kelly
St. Charles, MO

Keep it hot in a slow cooker or electric skillet...serve over
English muffins, biscuits or toast.

1/4 c. onion, chopped
1 T. butter
1 c. milk
8-oz. pkg. cream cheese,
    softened
1 c. dried, chipped beef

3-oz. can sliced mushrooms,
    drained
1/4 c. grated Parmesan cheese
2 T. fresh parsley, chopped
1/8 t. Worcestershire sauce

In a skillet over medium heat, sauté onion in butter until tender; stir in milk and cream cheese. Add remaining ingredients; heat until cheese melts. Makes about 3 cups.

Hearty in a **Hurry**

Beefy Tomato Rice Skillet

Erin Brock
Charleston, WV

So quick & easy to make using pantry staples!

1 lb. ground beef
1 c. celery, chopped
2/3 c. onion, chopped
1/2 c. green pepper, chopped
11-oz. can corn, drained

10-3/4 oz. can tomato soup
1 c. water
1 t. Italian seasoning
1 c. quick-cooking rice,
   uncooked

In a skillet over medium heat, cook beef, celery, onion and green pepper until meat is no longer pink and vegetables are tender; drain. Stir in corn, soup, water and Italian seasoning; bring to a boil. Stir in rice; cover and remove from heat. Let stand 10 minutes, or until rice is tender. Serves 6.

Make biscuits even better! Separate flaky layers and add mozzarella cheese and a little dried basil in between. Bake as usual for a cheesy treat.

Veggie Pizza Casserole

Alona Webb
Edgerton, WI

*A great way to serve up those zucchini that mysteriously appear
on your doorstep in late summer...your family will
never know that they're hidden in here!*

2 to 4 c. zucchini, shredded
1/2 t. salt
2 eggs, beaten
1/2 c. grated Parmesan cheese
1 c. shredded Cheddar cheese,
    divided
2 c. shredded mozzarella cheese,
    divided
1 lb. ground beef

3/4 c. sweet onion, chopped
15-oz. can tomato sauce
1/4 t. dried oregano
1/4 t. dried basil
1/2 t. garlic salt
1 T. fresh parsley, chopped
1 yellow or red pepper, chopped
1/4 c. olives, sliced

Place zucchini in a colander; sprinkle with salt and let drain well, squeezing out extra moisture. Add to a large bowl; stir in eggs, Parmesan cheese and half of each of the Cheddar and mozzarella cheeses. Spread into a greased 13"x9" baking pan. Bake, uncovered, at 400 degrees for 20 minutes. While baking, brown beef with onion in a skillet over medium heat; drain. Stir in tomato sauce and seasonings; heat thorough. Layer over baked zucchini; sprinkle with remaining cheeses. Arrange peppers and olives over top before serving. Serves 6 to 8.

Make Veggie Pizza Casserole with your favorite veggies. Try it with yellow squash, carrots or even eggplant. Just bake veggies in place of zucchini until tender and continue with recipe as usual. It'll be a summertime favorite!

Hearty in a Hurry

Pepperoni Calzones

Amy Greer
Elkhart, IN

No time to make dough? Make this yummy Italian dish with refrigerated pizza dough.

1 pkg. active dry yeast	1 egg, beaten
1 c. warm water	Garnish: pepperoni, green
1 T. sugar	pepper, mozzarella cheese
2 T. oil	and sliced mushrooms
1 t. salt	
3 to 3-1/4 c. all-purpose flour, divided	

In a bowl, dissolve yeast in very warm water, 110 to 115 degrees; let stand for 5 minutes. Stir in sugar, oil, salt and one cup flour; blend until smooth. Mix in enough remaining flour to make a smooth dough; knead on a lightly floured surface for 15 minutes. Place in a greased bowl; turn once. Cover and let rise until double in size, about 30 minutes. Punch dough down; divide into 6 equal parts. Roll each into a 7-inch circle; divide Tomato-Basil Sauce evenly and spread over dough to within one inch of its edge. Add desired garnishes to each; fold dough in half to cover filling and pinch edges to seal. Place on an ungreased baking sheet; let rest for 15 minutes. Brush with egg; bake at 350 degrees for 25 or 30 minutes, until golden. Makes 6.

Tomato-Basil Sauce:

8-oz. can tomato sauce	1 t. dried oregano
4-oz. can sliced mushrooms	1 clove garlic, minced
1 t. dried basil	

Combine ingredients together; mix well.

Ham & Green Bean Supper
Cathy McBride
Ashland, OH

A homestyle favorite that's always welcome at our table.

6 potatoes, peeled, cubed and
   boiled
2 14-1/2 oz. cans green beans,
   drained
1/2 c. onion, chopped

1 t. garlic powder
2 10-3/4 oz. cans cream of
   chicken soup
2 to 3 lbs. cooked ham, cubed
1/2 c. bread crumbs

In a bowl, combine all ingredients together except bread crumbs;
spread in a lightly greased 13"x9" baking pan. Sprinkle with bread
crumbs; bake, uncovered, at 350 degrees for 45 minutes. Serves 6.

Ham, Grapefruit &
Spinach Salad
Claire Bertram
Lexington, KY

When my girlfriends and I get together, we love trying new salad
combinations. This one's a keeper!

4 c. fresh spinach, torn
2 c. grapefruit segments
1/2 lb. deli ham, thinly sliced
   and cut into 1/2-inch strips
1 egg, hard-cooked, peeled and
   finely chopped

3 T. raspberry-flavored vinegar
3 T. honey
1-1/2 T. oil
2 t. Dijon mustard
1/8 t. pepper

Divide spinach among 4 serving plates. Top each with an equal
amount of grapefruit, ham and egg. In a bowl, whisk together
remaining ingredients. Drizzle over each serving plate. Serve
immediately. Serves 4.

Hearty in a Hurry

Cheesy Ham Strata

*Vivian Baker
Centerville, OH*

Put together the night before, it's great for celebrations and brunch!

12 slices bread, crusts trimmed
3/4 lb. Cheddar cheese, sliced
10-oz. pkg. frozen broccoli,
    thawed
2 c. cooked ham, cubed
2 T. dried, minced onion

6 eggs, beaten
3-1/2 c. milk
1/2 t. salt
1/4 t. dry mustard
1/2 c. shredded Cheddar cheese

Cut out desired shapes from center of each bread slice using cookie cutters; place shapes to the side and arrange remaining bread pieces in a greased 13"x9" baking pan. Layer cheese slices over bread pieces; spread broccoli and ham over cheese slices. Sprinkle with onion; arrange bread cut-outs on top. Blend eggs, milk, salt and mustard together; pour over the top. Cover and refrigerate overnight. Bake, uncovered, at 325 degrees until set, about 55 minutes. Sprinkle with shredded cheese for last 5 minutes of baking; let stand 10 minutes before serving. Makes 8 servings.

Serve crunchy Broccoli Salad on the side and everyone
is sure to ask for seconds! This classic recipe
can be found on page 46.

Simple Sloppy Joes

Jennifer Catterino
Pasadena, MD

Just as quick as using canned sauce!

1 lb. ground beef
1 onion, chopped
1 c. catsup
2 T. Worcestershire sauce
1/4 c. water
1/4 t. salt
1/4 t. pepper
6 to 8 sandwich buns, split

In a skillet, brown beef with onion; drain. Stir in catsup, Worcestershire sauce, water, salt and pepper. Simmer for 20 minutes, stirring frequently. Spoon onto buns. Makes 6 to 8.

Looking for a change from the everyday PB&J? Try spreading peanut butter and jelly on extra-large biscuits, flour tortillas or pita rounds. Other sandwich fillings work just as well too. Ham & cheese roll-ups are a quick & easy snack that can be eaten on the go!

Bacon-Wrapped Chicken, page 143

Sweet Potato Casserole, page 43

Chicken Taco Salad, page 23

Ham & Pineapple Kebobs, page 108

Triple Fudge Cake, page 199

Quick Salisbury Steak, page 138

Zesty Pizza Casserole, page 102

Easy Chicken Pot Pie, page 175

Pepper Steak, page115

Overnight Oriental Salad, page 56

White Chicken Pizza, page 21

Cinnamon Gingersnaps, page 195

Meatball Sub Casserole, page 104

Mesa Corn Pie, page 15

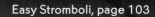
Easy Stromboli, page 103

Easy Cheesy Manicotti, page 57

Zippy Ziti & Broccoli, page 88

Carolyn's Chicken Tetrazzini, page 51

Zesty Macaroni & Cheese, page 60

Poppy Seed Chicken, page 147

Butterscotch Cheesecake Bars, page 200

BBQ Hamburgers

Kristin Freeman
Jenks, OK

A quick and tasty twist on a supper standard...kids love 'em!

2 lbs. ground beef	2 T. mustard
1/2 onion, chopped	2 T. brown sugar, packed
garlic salt and pepper to taste	1 T. vinegar
1 c. catsup	8 to 10 sandwich buns, split

In a skillet over medium heat, brown beef with onion and seasonings until onion is tender; drain. Combine catsup, mustard, brown sugar and vinegar in a small bowl; stir into beef mixture. Simmer for 30 minutes. Spoon onto buns to serve. Makes 8 to 10.

Sloppy Joe Casserole

Louise Fish
Shoreline, WA

A side of chips & dip and a big dill pickle
round out this speedy meal.

1 lb. ground beef	1 onion, chopped
2 potatoes, sliced	15-oz. can Sloppy Joe sauce

In a skillet over medium heat, brown beef; drain. Arrange potatoes on top; sprinkle with onion. Pour Sloppy Joe sauce over the mixture; simmer, covered, for 30 minutes. Makes 6 to 8 servings.

Save time by putting the food processor to work chopping and dicing veggies...so easy!

Beefy Supper Skillet

Karen Stoner
Delaware, OH

Water chestnuts add crunch to this fast family feast.

1 lb. ground beef
1/3 c. long-cooking rice,
    uncooked
1-oz. pkg. onion gravy mix
1/4 t. garlic salt

1-1/2 c. water
10-oz. pkg. frozen peas, thawed
5-oz. can water chestnuts
2.8-oz. can French fried onions
soy sauce to taste

In a skillet over medium heat, brown beef; drain. Add rice, gravy mix, garlic salt and water; bring to a boil. Reduce heat to low; cover and simmer for 15 minutes. Stir in peas and water chestnuts; simmer until rice is tender. Remove from heat; toss in onions. Season with soy sauce before serving. Serves 4 to 6.

Burger Beans with Apples

Dawn Slatem
Salem, OR

*We like this dish served over rice with a
thick slice of buttery garlic bread.*

1 lb. ground beef, browned
1 onion, chopped
15-oz. can tomato sauce
2 apples, cored, peeled
    and sliced

1/4 c. brown sugar, packed
2 15-1/2 oz. cans kidney beans,
    drained

Combine ingredients in a 2-quart casserole dish; bake, uncovered, at 325 degrees for 20 minutes. Makes 4 servings.

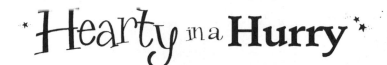

Hearty in a Hurry

Hamburger-Noodle Bake

Kate Conroy
Bethlehem, PA

A one-dish meal that is easy to make ahead of time and refrigerate for later...just heat it up when hunger hits!

1 lb. ground beef
1/2 c. onion, chopped
2 8-oz. cans tomato sauce
1 T. sugar
3/4 t. garlic salt
1/4 t. pepper

1 c. cottage cheese
1/4 c. sour cream
8-oz. pkg. cream cheese,
   softened
4 c. egg noodles, cooked
1/4 c. grated Parmesan cheese

In a skillet over medium heat, brown beef and onion; drain. Stir in tomato sauce, sugar, garlic salt and pepper; heat thorough. Remove from heat. In a large bowl, combine cottage cheese, sour cream and cream cheese; gently stir in noodles. Spread half the cheese mixture in an ungreased 13"x9" baking pan. Layer with half the beef mixture; repeat layers. Sprinkle with Parmesan cheese. Bake, uncovered, at 350 degrees for 30 minutes. Makes 8 servings.

Stuffed burgers turn ordinary into an extraordinary dinner! Form a thin beef patty and top with a sprinkle of cheese, roasted garlic, bacon crumbles, salsa or fresh herbs. Place another thin patty on top and carefully seal the edges. Grill as usual and enjoy!

Make-Ahead Ham Bites

Rosalie Elkins
Alton, IL

*These yummy little sandwiches make a filling
dinner...everyone's sure to ask for seconds!*

12 Hawaiian rolls, split
1 lb. deli ham, sliced
1/2 lb. Swiss cheese, sliced
3/4 c. butter, melted

1-1/2 t. Dijon mustard
1-1/2 t. Worcestershire sauce
1-1/2 t. dried, minced onion

Arrange bottoms of rolls in an ungreased 13"x9" baking pan; layer
ham and cheese on top. Replace tops of rolls. Whisk remaining
ingredients together; drizzle evenly over the rolls. Cover and refrigerate
overnight. Bake, uncovered, at 350 degrees for 15 to 20 minutes.
Makes 12 servings.

Hot Ham Sandwiches

Beth Feliciano
Wellington, OH

Delicious and easy to take along to family gatherings.

1/3 c. onion, minced
1/3 c. vinegar
2 t. mustard
2 T. Worcestershire sauce
1/8 t. salt

3 T. butter
1-1/2 c. brown sugar, packed
1/2 c. water
2 lbs. cooked ham, diced
10 Kaiser buns, split

In a skillet, combine all ingredients except ham and buns. Cook over
medium heat until onion is tender. Add ham; heat through. Spoon
onto buns to serve. Makes 8 to 10 servings.

Sausage-Kraut Skillet

Carol Lytle
Columbus, OH

I love sauerkraut and wanted a one-dish meal, so I came up with this tasty dish!

2 T. butter
1 onion, sliced
2 cloves garlic, minced
1 c. water
2 potatoes, peeled and sliced
1 c. carrots, peeled and sliced
2 T. beef bouillon granules
1 t. sugar

1/2 t. caraway seed
14-1/2 oz. can sauerkraut, drained
1 lb. Kielbasa sausage, sliced
2 t. all-purpose flour
1 c. sour cream
salt and pepper to taste

In a large skillet with a lid, melt butter over medium heat. Cook onion and garlic until onion is translucent, about 5 minutes. Stir in water, potatoes, carrot, bouillon granules, sugar and caraway seed; bring to a boil. Reduce heat to low; simmer, stirring occasionally, until potatoes and carrots are tender, about 15 minutes. Layer sauerkraut over vegetables in skillet; add sausage on top. Cover and cook until heated through, about 15 minutes. In a bowl, whisk flour into sour cream; add to skillet and mix well. Simmer until thickened; add salt and pepper to taste. Serve warm. Serves 6.

Laughter is brightest where food is best.
–Irish Proverb

Beefy Onion Bake

Debbie Watson
Maumelle, AR

*Baking time allows just enough time to read the paper
and help the kids finish their homework.*

1 lb. ground beef
10-3/4 oz. can cream of
    mushroom soup
10-3/4 oz. can cream of
    celery soup
10-3/4 oz. can cream of
    chicken soup

1-1/2 oz. pkg. dry onion soup
    mix
2 c. instant rice, uncooked
1-1/2 c. water

In a skillet over medium heat, brown beef until no longer pink; drain.
Add remaining ingredients; spread in an ungreased 13"x9" baking pan.
Bake, covered, at 325 degrees for 45 minutes, or until hot and bubbly.
Makes 8 servings.

Dinner in a Pinch

Kim Mangum
Abilene, TX

*My kids call this their all-time favorite...if they only knew that
I made it up one day from what was left in the pantry!*

1 lb. ground beef
2 potatoes, peeled and sliced
14-1/2 oz. can tomatoes with
    green chiles

14-1/2-oz. can green beans
1/4 c. onion, chopped
1 stalk celery, sliced
salt and pepper to taste

In a skillet over medium heat, brown beef until no longer pink; drain.
Add remaining ingredients; stir gently. Simmer until potatoes are
tender, about 20 minutes. Makes 4 servings.

Wagon Wheel Skillet

June LeBeau
Alpena, MI

I serve in wedges right from the skillet...it looks just like a wagon wheel!

1 T. dried, minced onion
1/2 c. milk
1-1/2 lbs. ground beef
1 egg, beaten
1/2 c. quick-cooking oats,
   uncooked
2 t. salt

1/4 t. pepper
browning and seasoning sauce
   to taste
1 c. spaghetti sauce with
   mushrooms
1 c. kidney beans

In a large bowl, soak onion in milk for 5 minutes; mix in beef, egg, oats, salt and pepper. Mound in a large skillet; score into 5 or 6 wedges. Brush tops lightly with browning sauce; set aside. Combine spaghetti sauce and kidney beans; pour over meat. Simmer over medium heat, uncovered, until cooked through and no longer pink, about 25 to 30 minutes. Serves 5 to 6.

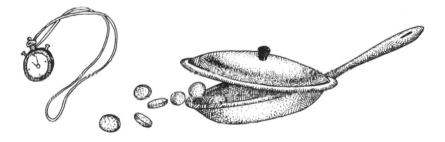

Make clean-up a snap! Before dinner even starts,
fill the sink with hot, soapy water. Put dishes right in
when cooking's finished and, by the time
dessert is eaten, they'll be a breeze to wash!

Deli Stromboli

Anna Thompson
Mechanicsburg, PA

Serve with a side of warmed marinara sauce.

2 10-oz. tubes refrigerated
   pizza crust
1/2 lb. deli ham, sliced
   and divided
1/4 lb. hard salami, sliced
1/4 lb. pepperoni, sliced

1/4 lb. mozzarella cheese, sliced
1/4 lb. provolone cheese, sliced
1/4 lb. American cheese, sliced
1 c. sliced mushrooms
1/3 c. hot pepper rings
1 onion, sliced

Roll crusts out on a lightly greased baking sheet to completely cover
the bottom. Layer 1/4 pound meat, a cheese and then a vegetable;
continue for 3 layers, ending with a layer of remaining ham. Fold
dough back over top, envelope-style; pinch edges closed, making sure
all ingredients are tucked inside. Bake at 425 degrees until golden,
about 17 to 25 minutes; let stand 5 to 10 minutes before slicing.
Serves 8.

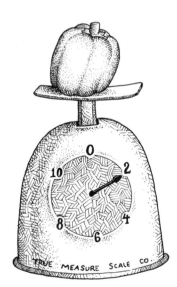

Brush melted butter over this
Deli Stromboli, sprinkle on
Italian seasoning and some
grated Parmesan cheese
before baking. Extra tasty!

Parmesan Meatballs

Karen Mihok
Valencia, CA

My children loved this dish growing up and now,
my grandsons love it too.

1 to 1-1/2 lbs. ground beef
1/2 c. grated Parmesan cheese
1/2 c. bread crumbs
2 T. dried, minced onion
1 egg
1 c. milk, divided

2 to 4 T. butter
1/4 c. all-purpose flour
10-1/2 oz. can beef broth
1/2 c. dry white wine or
　beef broth

In a large bowl, mix beef, Parmesan cheese, bread crumbs, onion, egg and 1/2 cup milk; shape into 1-1/2 or 2-inch balls. Sauté in butter in a large, heavy skillet over medium heat; remove meatballs to a platter when browned. Decrease heat to low; whisk flour into drippings in skillet. Increase heat to medium and gradually whisk in remaining milk, broth and wine or broth; bring to a boil until mixture thickens, stirring often. Return meatballs to skillet; reduce heat, cover and simmer for 20 minutes. Serves 4 to 6.

Make baked meatballs even more special...press a cube
of fresh mozzarella inside them before baking.
Yummy and oh-so cheesy!

Quick Salisbury Steak

Alma Meyers
Guernsey, WY

Add a side of mashed potatoes for a hearty, filling dinner.

1 lb. ground beef
1-1/2 oz. pkg. onion soup mix
2 eggs, beaten

2 10-3/4 oz. cans golden
  mushroom soup

In a large bowl, combine beef, soup mix and eggs; mix well and form into 4 patties. Place patties in an ungreased 13"x9" baking pan; cover with soup. Bake at 350 degrees for 35 minutes, or until patties are no longer pink in the center. Makes 4 servings.

When freezing ground beef, why not brown it first? Add
seasoning, drain and cool before placing recipe-sized
servings into freezer bags...they'll be ready for
all those meals in minutes!

Quick
as a Wink

Chicken 'n Cheese Pie

Marilyn Williams
Westerville, OH

This is the first recipe I passed on to my daughter
after she got married...it's a family favorite.

1-1/2 c. medium egg noodles,
    cooked
2 c. shredded Cheddar cheese
5-oz. can evaporated milk
2 5-oz. cans chicken, drained
    and chopped

2 drops hot pepper sauce
4-oz. jar chopped pimentos,
    drained
1/4 t. garlic salt
10-inch deep-dish pie crust
1/8 t. paprika

Combine all ingredients together except pie crust and paprika; mix gently. Arrange crust in a 10" pie plate. Spread noodle mixture into pie crust; set on a baking sheet. Sprinkle with paprika; bake at 400 degrees until golden, about 25 minutes. Let cool 15 minutes before serving. Makes 6 servings.

Turn refrigerated dinner rolls into a pull-apart treat
at dinnertime. Pull the rolls apart into four pieces and
place them in a plastic zipping bag with cheese and
some zesty seasonings...shake 'em up, pile into
a greased casserole dish and bake as usual.

Quick as a Wink

Crispy Potato-Chicken

Cindy Mansfield
Cary, NC

*A new favorite in our house...my mom made this dish one night
while we were visiting and my husband just flipped over it!*

1 lb. boneless, skinless chicken
   breasts
2 T. Dijon mustard
1/2 t. clove garlic, chopped

1 potato, grated
1/2 t. oil
1/2 t. lemon juice
1 t. pepper

Arrange chicken breasts in a 9"x9" baking pan that has been lightly
sprayed with non-stick vegetable spray; set aside. Combine mustard
and garlic; spread over chicken breasts and set aside. Mix potato, oil
and lemon juice; spread over chicken breasts. Sprinkle with pepper;
bake, uncovered, at 425 degrees for 25 to 35 minutes or until juices
run clear when pierced with a fork. Serves 2 to 4.

Buying boneless, skinless chicken breasts in bulk? Grill or
pan-fry them all at once. Season with salt, pepper and garlic,
if desired, and allow to cool. Wrap tightly in plastic wrap or
place in a freezer bag. Kept in the freezer, they'll be ready
for quick lunches, chicken salad or zesty fajitas!

Sesame-Plum Chicken

Bernadette Bader
Beverly, OH

*Baking time depends on thickness and number of chicken breasts...
always pierce and check for doneness before serving.*

6 T. all-purpose flour
2 T. cornstarch
2 eggs, beaten
2 t. salt
4 to 6 boneless, skinless chicken
    breasts

1 c. bread crumbs
1/2 c. sesame seed
1/2 c. butter
1/2 c. oil

Combine flour, cornstarch, eggs and salt in a shallow pie plate; dip chicken breasts in mixture. Coat with bread crumbs; sprinkle with sesame seed and set aside. Heat butter and oil in a heavy skillet; brown chicken breasts on both sides. Transfer to an ungreased 13"x9" baking pan; bake, uncovered, at 350 degrees for 20 to 40 minutes, until juices run clear when pierced with a fork. Remove to a serving plate; spoon Plum Sauce over top. Makes 4 to 6 servings.

Plum Sauce:

1 c. red plum preserves
1/2 c. apricot preserves
1/2 c. applesauce

1/4 c. vinegar
2 T. honey
1/2 c. cranberry sauce

Stir ingredients together in a heavy saucepan; simmer until heated through. Serve warm.

Reserve a few tablespoons of Plum Sauce to stir into
some prepared wild rice blend. Sprinkle with sesame seed
and heat through for a speedy side dish.

Bacon-Wrapped Chicken

Linda Strausburg
Arroyo Grande, CA

Each chicken breast is coated with herb-flavored cream cheese, rolled up and wrapped in bacon, making this dish an excellent choice for special get-togethers!

2 boneless, skinless chicken
    breasts, flattened to 1/2-inch
    thickness
1/2 t. salt
1/4 t. pepper

2 T. chive-and-onion-flavored
    cream cheese, softened
    and divided
2 T. chilled butter, divided
1/2 t. dried tarragon, divided
2 slices bacon

Sprinkle chicken with salt and pepper. Spread one tablespoon cream cheese over each chicken breast; top with one tablespoon butter and 1/4 teaspoon tarragon. Roll up and wrap with one slice bacon; secure with a toothpick. Place chicken seam-side down on an ungreased baking sheet. Bake at 400 degrees for 30 minutes or until juices run clear when pierced with a fork. Increase tempature to broil. Watching the broiler carefully, broil 8 to 10 minutes or just until bacon is crisp. Makes 2 servings.

Here's an easy sauce that's just right spooned over
Bacon-Wrapped Chicken. Melt a tablespoon of butter
and stir in 3 tablespoons Dijon or honey mustard...
sweet, tangy and oh-so good.

Chicken Tortilla Soup

Robie Coleman
Piedmont, OK

I explained to my mother-in-law that I didn't think I could manage a recipe with more than six ingredients. With her encouragement, we simplified her recipe for this soup and it turned out delicious!

28-oz. can diced tomatoes
14-oz. can corn
14-1/2 oz. can black beans
4-oz. can diced green chiles
2 14-1/2 oz. cans chicken broth
1-3/4 c. water
2 chicken bouillon cubes
1 to 2 T. dried, minced onion
1 clove garlic, minced

1 t. ground cumin
salt and pepper to taste
2 boneless, skinless chicken
   breasts, cooked and cubed
6 to 8 tortillas, cut into 1/4-inch
   strips
Garnish: shredded Cheddar
   cheese

Add all ingredients except chicken, tortillas and cheese to a heavy stockpot. Bring to a boil; reduce heat and simmer 20 minutes. Add chicken; cook 10 minutes. Broil tortilla strips until toasted, stirring often. Ladle soup into bowls; sprinkle with tortilla strips and cheese. Makes 8 servings.

When making homemade soups and stews, save a few spoonfuls of the broth to freeze in ice cube trays. Add them to vegetables or rice later for a flavor punch!

Chicken Enchilada Casserole *Chrissy Boyd*
Collinsville, OK

I first tasted this dish at a church supper. I liked it so much, I went around the room with the empty pan asking who had brought it. Thank you Mrs. Hampton for a new family favorite!

1 onion, chopped
1/2 c. margarine
10-3/4 oz. can cream of
  chicken soup
10-3/4 oz. can cream of
  mushroom soup
4-1/2 oz. can chopped green
  chiles

1 c. chicken broth
6 to 8 flour tortillas, torn into
  bite-size pieces and divided
4 boneless, skinless chicken
  breasts, cooked and cubed
1/2 lb. Cheddar cheese, sliced

Sauté onion in margarine in a heavy skillet until tender; add soups, chiles and broth, mixing well. Layer half the tortilla pieces in a 13"x9" baking pan that has been sprayed with non-stick vegetable spray. Layer chicken, cheese slices and remaining tortilla pieces on top; pour on soup mixture. Bake, uncovered, at 350 degrees for 30 minutes, or until heated through. Makes 6 servings.

Pair these up with Chile-Cheese 'Taters (on page 15) for a homemade fiesta that's sure to please!

Summer Raspberry Chicken

Merrill Reid
Dundee, MI

Serve on fresh greens or a bed of angel hair pasta and garnish with fresh raspberries...delicious!

4 boneless, skinless chicken
    breasts
3/4 c. Dijon and honey marinade
    with lemon juice, divided

1 c. raspberries
1/2 c. chopped walnuts

Pound chicken breasts to 1/4-inch thickness; coat and baste with 1/2 cup marinade. Broil or grill until juices run clear when chicken is pierced with a fork, turning once and basting often but not during last 5 minutes of cooking time. Discard basting marinade; cut chicken into strips and set aside. Process raspberries and remaining 1/4 cup marinade in a blender for 10 seconds; drizzle over chicken. Sprinkle with walnuts; serve warm. Makes 4 to 6 servings.

Add a splash of color to sparkling cider and lemonade.
Freeze grape or cranberry juice in ice cube trays and
add a few to drinking glasses...so pretty!

Poppy Seed Chicken

Connie Gabbard
Athens, OH

*Don't be tempted to sprinkle on the cracker-crumb mixture
while the chicken is in the slow cooker...condensation will make
the topping soggy.*

6 boneless, skinless chicken
   breasts
2 10-3/4 oz. cans cream of
   chicken soup
1 c. milk

1 T. poppy seed
36 round buttery crackers,
   crushed
1/4 c. butter, melted

Place chicken in a lightly greased 5-quart slow cooker. Whisk together soup, milk and poppy seed in a bowl; spoon over chicken. Cover and cook on high setting for one hour. Reduce heat to low setting; cover and cook for 3 hours. Combine cracker crumbs and butter in a bowl, stirring until crumbs are moistened. Sprinkle over chicken just before serving. Serves 6.

Freeze chicken breasts or pork chops with their marinades
in airtight containers. By the time it's frozen and thawed
for cooking, the meat will have absorbed just enough
flavor...so easy and delicious!

Bea's Turkey Casserole

Jody McKeown
Coloma, MI

*Gobbles up any turkey leftovers...I remember it because
Mom made it only a few times a year!*

2-1/2 c. cooked turkey, cubed
10-3/4 oz. can cream of
    mushroom soup
2 stalks celery, diced
1 onion, diced
3/4 c. mayonnaise-type salad
    dressing

1/2 c. chopped pecans
2 c. potato chips, crushed
3 eggs, hard-boiled, peeled
    and chopped
lemon pepper and salt to taste

Mix all ingredients together; stir gently. Spread in an ungreased
2-quart casserole dish; bake, uncovered, at 350 degrees for 30 to
40 minutes, or until hot and bubbly. Serves 4.

Turkey Shepherd's Pie

Leah Wicker
Chattanooga, TN

Quick, easy and scrumptious!

1 lb. ground turkey
1 onion, chopped
2 c. brown gravy

8 slices American cheese
4 c. mashed potatoes

In a skillet over medium heat, brown turkey with onion; drain. Place
in a greased 2-quart casserole dish. Pour gravy over turkey; top with
cheese and mashed potatoes. Bake, uncovered, at 350 degrees for
20 minutes, or until hot and bubbly. Serves 4.

Maple-Cranberry Turkey

Delinda Blakney
Scotts Hill, TN

Just right for chilly autumn evenings.

1-lb. pkg. turkey breast
   tenderloins
1/3 c. sweetened, dried
   cranberries
1/4 c. orange juice

1/3 c. maple syrup
1 T. butter
1/4 t. cinnamon
23-oz. can sweet potatoes,
   drained

Brown turkey in a skillet over medium heat; set aside. In a saucepan, heat cranberries, orange juice, syrup, butter and cinnamon until boiling; remove from heat. Add sweet potatoes to the turkey tenderloins in the skillet; pour cranberry mixture over top. Cover and cook over low heat for 10 minutes; uncover and cook until sauce thickens, about 5 more minutes. Makes 4 servings.

Fresh sweet potatoes can easily be used in place of canned.
Just cut them into bite-size pieces and microwave
for five minutes or until tender. Peel each piece and
add to recipe as usual.

Jamaican Marinade

Kristen Blanton
Big Bear City, CA

Marinate chicken for two to three hours before grilling.

1/3 c. olive oil
3 T. white vinegar
1-1/2 T. lime juice
1 T. sugar
1/4 c. green onions, minced
2 cloves garlic, minced

1 jalapeño, seeded and chopped
1 t. dried thyme
3/4 t. allspice
1/2 t. cinnamon
1/2 t. salt
cayenne pepper to taste

Combine all ingredients; mix well. Makes enough marinade for 2 pounds of chicken.

Lemon-Lime Marinade

Nora Rausch
Hurleyville, NY

Marinate chicken in this tangy sauce overnight then grill or broil...your family will ask for more!

1/2 c. brown sugar, packed
3 T. Dijon mustard
1/4 c. cider vinegar
juice of one lime

juice of one lemon
6 T. olive oil
pepper to taste

Whisk ingredients together. Makes enough marinade for 2 pounds of chicken.

Before marinating chicken, reserve some marinade in a plastic squeeze bottle for easy basting...how clever!

Quick as a Wink

Crunchy Chicken Salad

Leigh Ann Huber
Cypress, TX

Serve with baked wonton chips.

1-lb. pkg. boneless, skinless
  chicken breasts, chopped
2 T. oil
12-oz. pkg. coleslaw mix
2 carrots, peeled and grated
2 to 3 green onions, chopped

fresh cilantro to taste, chopped
1/4 c. sunflower seeds
1/4 c. toasted, sliced almonds
2 3-oz. pkgs. chicken-flavored
  ramen noodles with
  seasoning packets

Sauté chicken in oil until golden and juices run clear when pierced with a fork; drain and cool. In a large serving bowl, combine chicken with remaining ingredients except ramen noodles; mix well. Crumble uncooked ramen noodles, reserving seasoning packets for dressing; stir in. Pour Dressing on top just before serving; toss gently. Serves 4 to 6.

Dressing:

2 T. sugar
1 t. pepper
3/4 to 1 c. oil

7 T. rice vinegar
2 ramen noodle seasoning
  packets

Whisk ingredients together.

Mix up the ingredients for this quick & easy salad in a plastic zipping bag and it'll be done in half the time. Just blend by shaking and spoon out individual servings.

Chicken & Rice Casserole *Juliah Humphreys*
Cleveland, TN

So easy and versatile...it's even better the next day.

4 to 5 boneless, skinless chicken
   breasts, cooked and cubed
14-1/2 oz. can French-style
   green beans
1 c. mayonnaise
8-oz. can sliced water chestnuts,
   drained

10-3/4 oz. can cream of
   celery soup
6.9-oz. pkg. chicken-flavored
   rice vermicelli mix, cooked
salt and pepper to taste
Garnish: grated Parmesan
   cheese

Combine all ingredients together; spread in an ungreased 13"x9" baking pan. Bake, uncovered, at 350 degrees until golden, about 30 to 45 minutes. Serves 8.

Soda-Pop Chicken

LynnMarie Frucci
La Center, WA

Serve with corn on the cob...kids love it!

6 boneless, skinless chicken
   breasts
2 T. oil

12-oz. can cola
18-oz. bottle barbecue sauce

In a skillet over medium heat, cook chicken in oil until juices run clear when pierced with a fork. Stir in cola and barbecue sauce. Reduce heat; simmer 30 to 40 minutes. Serves 6.

Quick as a Wink

Momma's Divine Divan

Marsha Reid
Pasadena, CA

The ingredients are almost always on hand!

1/2 lb. broccoli flowerets, cooked
4 to 5 boneless, skinless chicken
    breasts, cooked and cubed
1 c. seasoned bread crumbs
1 T. butter, melted
10-3/4 oz. can cream of
    chicken soup

1/2 t. lemon juice
1/2 t. curry powder
1/2 c. mayonnaise
1 c. shredded Cheddar cheese

Arrange broccoli in the bottom of an ungreased 13"x9" baking pan; place chicken on top and set aside. In a bowl, toss bread crumbs and butter together; set aside. Combine soup, lemon juice, curry powder and mayonnaise; spoon over chicken and broccoli. Top with cheese; sprinkle with bread crumb mixture. Bake, uncovered, at 350 degrees for 25 minutes. Makes 8 to 10 servings.

Fresh out of bread crumbs for this crunchy topping?
Use herb-flavored stuffing mix instead and
it'll be just as yummy!

Chicken with Sorrel Sauce

Cindy Vitko
Huntington, CT

Sorrel has a tangy citrus-lemon flavor...a perfect herbal
complement to poultry or fish dishes.

2 boneless, skinless chicken
   breasts, halved
2 T. margarine, divided
1 t. dried tarragon
6 to 7 sorrel leaves

1/2 c. sour cream
3/4 c. light cream
2 t. dried parsley
1/2 t. dried rosemary
salt and pepper to taste

In a skillet over medium heat, cook chicken in one tablespoon
margarine until juices run clear when pierced with a fork; sprinkle
with tarragon and set aside. Melt remaining margarine in a saucepan;
add sorrel, stirring until just wilted. Add sour cream, cream, parsley,
rosemary, salt and pepper; reduce heat and cook until warmed
through. Do not boil. Arrange chicken in an ungreased 8"x8" baking
pan; pour sauce on top. Bake, uncovered, at 350 degrees for
30 minutes. Serves 2.

Substitute any summer greens for sorrel in this recipe.
Mustard greens, collards or even spinach
will work well too.

Quick as a Wink

Chicken & Wild Rice

Marion Pfeifer
Smyrna, DE

*Our church has many covered-dish dinners and this recipe
came from one of the best cooks in our congregation!*

6-oz. pkg. long-grain and wild
    rice with seasonings
1/2 lb. sliced mushrooms
2 T. butter
2 c. chicken, cooked and diced

1/2 c. sour cream
10-3/4 oz. can cream of
    mushroom soup

Prepare rice according to package directions; set aside. In a skillet over medium heat, sauté mushrooms in butter until tender; add rice and remaining ingredients. Mix gently; spread in an ungreased 2-quart casserole dish. Bake, uncovered, at 350 degrees for 30 minutes. Serves 4.

Grilling bone-in chicken? Rub dry spices under the skin
if desired but leave the skin on while cooking...it keeps
moisture in. Also, wait until the last few minutes of
cooking time to brush on sauces for the best flavor.

155

Simple Mozzarella Chicken
Linda Wallace
Elwood, IN

So quick and impressive enough for company!

6 boneless, skinless chicken
   breasts
2 eggs, beaten
1 c. Italian-style bread crumbs
2 T. oil

2 15-oz. cans crushed tomatoes
   with green peppers
1-1/2 c. shredded mozzarella
   cheese
Garnish: chopped fresh basil

Dip chicken in eggs; coat with bread crumbs. Heat oil in a skillet; cook chicken over medium heat until juices run clear when pierced with a fork. Remove from heat. Spread one can of tomatoes in a greased 13"x9" baking pan; arrange chicken on top. Pour remaining can of tomatoes over chicken breasts; sprinkle with cheese. Bake, uncovered, at 375 degrees for 25 minutes; sprinkle with basil before serving. Serves 6.

A quick & easy side dish! Roll balls of leftover mashed potatoes in a mixture of Parmesan cheese and seasoned bread crumbs...broil until golden.

Quick as a Wink

Coconut Chicken

Dee Nargi
Chelmsford, MA

Look for Caribbean dipping sauces in the international aisle.

1/2 c. milk
3 eggs, beaten
3/4 c. all-purpose flour
7-oz. pkg. flaked coconut
salt and pepper to taste

2 to 3 boneless, skinless chicken
  breasts, cut into bite-size
  pieces
oil for deep frying

Blend milk and eggs together; whisk in flour until smooth. Add coconut, salt and pepper. Dip chicken in mixture; deep-fry in 365-degree oil until golden and juices run clear when pierced with a fork, about 15 minutes. Drain on paper towels. Makes 2 to 3 servings.

Swiss Chicken & Stuffing

Jeannette Stewart
Florissant, CO

Seasoned stuffing makes this dish twice as easy!

4 to 6 boneless, skinless chicken
  breasts
4 to 6 slices Swiss cheese
10-3/4 oz. can cream of
  chicken soup

1/4 c. water
2 c. herb-flavored stuffing mix
1/3 c. butter, melted

Arrange chicken in an ungreased 2-quart casserole dish. Place one slice of cheese on each piece of chicken. Combine soup and water; spoon evenly over chicken. Sprinkle stuffing mix over the top; drizzle with melted butter. Bake, uncovered, at 350 degrees for 35 minutes. Serves 4 to 6.

Chicken & Chips

Katherine Abbamont
Princeton, NJ

Prepared ahead of time, it's so easy to pop in the oven for dinner!

4 c. cooked chicken, diced
3/4 c. mayonnaise
10-3/4 oz. can cream of
   chicken soup
2 c. celery, chopped
4 eggs, hard-boiled, peeled
   and chopped

1 t. salt
1 t. onion, chopped
2 t. lemon juice
1 c. potato chips, crushed
2/3 c. shredded Cheddar cheese

In a large bowl, combine chicken with remaining ingredients except crushed chips and cheese; spread in a lightly greased 13"x9" baking pan. Toss crushed chips and cheese together; spread evenly over chicken mixture. Cover with aluminum foil; refrigerate 8 hours to overnight. Bake, uncovered, at 400 degrees until golden, about 25 minutes. Serves 4 to 6.

A new twist on casserole toppers...try crushed
flavored crackers combined with fresh or dried herbs.

Chicken Primavera

Corinne Vogel
Washington, IA

*Try this dish with your favorite kind of pasta or whatever's
on hand in the pantry!*

16-oz. pkg. angel hair pasta
1 onion, chopped
1 c. sliced mushrooms
1 green pepper, chopped
2 T. butter

1 to 2 c. Italian salad dressing,
   divided
2 boneless, skinless chicken
   breasts, cooked and chopped
1 tomato, chopped

Prepare pasta according to package directions; drain. In a skillet over
medium heat, sauté onion, mushrooms and green pepper in butter
with 2 tablespoons dressing until vegetables are tender. Reduce heat.
Add chicken and tomato; heat until warmed through. Toss with pasta;
stir in remaining dressing to taste. Serve warm. Serves 4 to 6.

Give bagels a turn at the table...instead of dinner rolls,
serve up toasted bagels with savory cream cheese
or a melted slice of cheese. Yum!

Turkey Pizza Sandwiches

Tina Stidam
Delaware, OH

Parmesan cheese is yummy sprinkled on top too.

2 T. olive oil
4 turkey breast fillets
1/2 c. Italian salad dressing
4 kaiser rolls

2 T. butter
garlic powder to taste
8-oz. jar pizza sauce, divided
1 c. shredded mozzarella cheese

Heat olive oil in a large non-stick skillet over medium-high heat. Coat turkey fillets with Italian dressing; brown for 6 to 8 minutes or until juices run clear when pierced with a fork. Remove from heat; set aside. Split rolls in half; lightly butter each half. Sprinkle halves with garlic powder; broil until just golden. Spread one tablespoon pizza sauce on bottom halves of rolls; top each with a turkey fillet and another tablespoon of sauce. Sprinkle with cheese; broil to melt cheese. Add top halves of rolls; serve with remaining sauce and cheese. Makes 4.

Host pizza night and make dinnertime fun! Use English muffins, pita rounds, bagels or tortillas for the crusts. Set out some ready-made pizza sauce, plenty of cheese and toppings in individual bowls. While the pizzas are baking, gather everyone 'round for a quick game of charades!

BBQ Turkey Meatballs

Paula Lydzinski
Perkasie, PA

I served a double recipe of these meatballs to three adults and one child...there were only four left after lunch. They're so good!

1 lb. ground turkey
1 onion, minced
1 egg, beaten
1/2 c. bread crumbs
1 T. milk
1 t. salt

1 c. catsup
1 clove garlic, minced
1/2 c. brown sugar, packed
1/4 c. lemon juice
3 T. Worcestershire sauce
salt and pepper to taste

In a bowl, combine turkey, onion, egg, bread crumbs, milk and salt; mix well. Form into 24 balls; set aside. Add remaining ingredients to a Dutch oven; bring to a boil over medium heat. Add meatballs; cover and simmer until fully cooked, about 20 to 25 minutes. Serves 4.

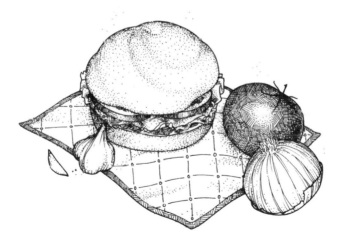

Make meatball subs for a hearty dinner on the go. Pack BBQ Turkey Meatballs, sliced cheese, lettuce, tomato and sub buns...perfect for a picnic in the park!

Turkey Joes

Glenda Oakley
Huron, SD

If you're in a big hurry, just use store-bought BBQ sauce.

3 c. cooked turkey, shredded
1/2 c. onion, chopped
1/2 c. barbecue sauce

1 T. mustard
salt and pepper to taste
8 kaiser rolls

Combine all ingredients except rolls in a saucepan; heat until warm. Spoon heaping spoonfuls onto rolls to serve. Makes 8.

Barbecue Sauce:

1 c. catsup
1 T. Dijon mustard
1 t. beef bouillon granules
2 t. chili powder

1 T. garlic salt
2 T. Worcestershire sauce
2 T. brown sugar, packed
1 T. lemon juice

Stir ingredients together in a saucepan; bring to a boil. Reduce heat; simmer on low for 15 minutes, stirring occasionally. Store in refrigerator in an airtight container. Makes 1-1/2 cups.

Make banana pops for a frosty treat to enjoy after Turkey Joes! Peel a banana and spread with fruit-flavored yogurt, sprinkle with nuts and place on a baking sheet to freeze. Once frozen, wrap in plastic wrap and enjoy a cool snack now or anytime.

Hearty Turkey Chili

Carla Marcinek
Huntington Beach, CA

Make a pan of cornbread or a sheet of cornbread twists
to enjoy on the side.

1 lb. ground turkey, browned
1 onion, chopped
15-1/2 oz. can kidney beans,
   drained
15-oz. can corn, drained
1 c. celery, chopped

1 T. chili powder
1 t. salt
14-1/2 oz. can diced tomatoes
pepper to taste
Garnish: shredded Cheddar
   cheese

Combine all ingredients except garnish in a stockpot; cook over medium heat until celery is tender and mixture is warmed through. Spoon into bowls; garnish with cheese. Makes 4 to 6 servings.

Next to jazz music, there is nothing that lifts the spirit and strengthens the soul more than a good bowl of chili.

–Harry James

Macadamia Nut Chicken

Linda Patten
Lake Zurich, IL

So tender you can cut it with a fork...yum!

3/4 c. bread crumbs
2/3 c. macadamia nuts, chopped
1/4 t. salt
2 boneless, skinless chicken
    breasts, flattened to 1/4-inch
    thickness

1 egg, beaten
2 T. butter
2 T. olive oil

Combine bread crumbs, macadamia nuts and salt together on a plate; set aside. Dip chicken in egg; coat with bread crumb mixture. Brown both sides in butter and oil in a skillet over medium-high heat; reduce heat to low and cover. Cook until juices run clear when chicken is pierced with a fork, about 5 to 7 minutes. Serves 2.

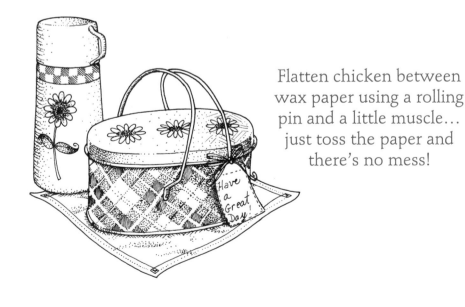

Flatten chicken between wax paper using a rolling pin and a little muscle... just toss the paper and there's no mess!

Parmesan Chicken

*Irene Robinson
Cincinnati, OH*

Takes so little time to prepare and looks so pretty on the table.

1/2 c. seasoned bread crumbs
1/4 c. grated Parmesan cheese
1/2 t. dried basil
4 boneless, skinless chicken
    breasts, flattened to 1/4-inch
    thickness

1 egg, beaten
1 T. butter
1 T. oil

In a shallow bowl, combine bread crumbs, Parmesan cheese and basil. Dip chicken into egg; coat with bread crumb mixture. In a skillet over medium heat, brown chicken in butter and oil for 3 to 5 minutes on each side, or until juices run clear when pierced with a fork. Makes 4 servings.

Kathie's Can-Can Chicken

*Nancy Gray
Farmington Hills, MI*

This recipe is from my sister Kathie's special collection...our whole family looks forward to eating at her house.

10-3/4 oz. can cream of
    chicken soup
10-3/4 oz. can cream of
    celery soup
1-1/4 c. water

1-1/3 c. instant rice, uncooked
1-1/2 c. chicken, cooked and
    diced
3-oz. can chow mein noodles

Combine all ingredients except chow mein noodles in a large skillet; bring to a boil. Reduce heat to low; simmer, covered, for 7 minutes. Place chow mein noodles in an ungreased 2-quart casserole dish; spread chicken mixture on top. Bake, uncovered, at 350 degrees for 10 to 15 minutes. Serves 4.

Chicken-Noodle Casserole

Sherre Klink
Roanoke, VA

Homebaked goodness in 20 minutes!

8-oz. pkg. wide egg noodles
1/2 c. butter, divided
1/3 c. all-purpose flour
2 c. chicken broth
3/4 c. milk
Optional: 1/4 c. white wine

2 t. salt
1/2 t. pepper
1 c. sliced mushrooms
2 c. cooked chicken, diced
1/3 c. grated Parmesan cheese

Prepare noodles according to package directions; drain. Melt 1/4 cup butter in a large saucepan over medium heat; whisk in flour, broth and milk until smooth and thickened. Add wine, if using, salt and pepper; set aside. In a skillet over medium heat, sauté mushrooms in remaining butter until tender; add to saucepan. Fold in noodles and chicken; pour into a greased 2-quart casserole dish. Sprinkle with Parmesan cheese. Bake, uncovered, at 350 degrees until hot and bubbly, about 20 minutes. Makes 6 servings.

Enjoy homemade veggie soup anytime! Just pour chicken or beef broth into individual airtight containers, toss in frozen mixed vegetables and cooked noodles. Freeze until needed and thaw in the microwave...ready in a snap.

South Carolina Gumbo

Rachel Reilly
Columbia, SC

The taste of the South in a hearty stew.

2 c. boneless, skinless chicken
   breasts, cubed
2 c. okra, chopped
2 14-1/2 oz. cans chicken broth
1 c. water
14-1/2 oz. can diced tomatoes
1 onion, chopped

1 stalk celery, sliced
1/2 green pepper, chopped
1/4 t. garlic powder
1 t. Cajun seasoning
salt and pepper to taste
1 c. instant rice, uncooked

Combine all ingredients except rice in a stockpot; bring to a boil.
Reduce heat and simmer, covered, for 15 minutes or until juices from
chicken run clear when pierced with a fork. Add rice; simmer, covered,
15 more minutes, or until rice is tender. Serves 6.

No Cajun seasoning on hand? Mix together 1/2 teaspoon
each black pepper, white pepper, garlic powder, onion
powder, ground cayenne pepper and paprika.

Jay's Favorite Chicken

Darlene Carter
Nashua, NH

This is my husband's favorite...serve with
mashed potatoes and steamed fresh broccoli.

4 boneless, skinless chicken
    breasts
4 slices Swiss cheese
10-3/4 oz. can cream of
    broccoli soup

1/2 c. milk
1 c. herb-flavored stuffing mix,
    crushed
1/4 c. butter, melted

Arrange chicken breasts in a greased 13"x9" baking pan; top with cheese slices. Combine soup and milk; pour over chicken. Toss stuffing crumbs and butter together; sprinkle over chicken. Bake, uncovered, at 350 degrees for 45 minutes. Makes 4 servings.

The next time mashed potatoes are on the dinner menu, whip in a teaspoon or so of baking powder and they'll be extra light and fluffy...don't forget the butter!

Chicken Stir-Fry

Jo Ann
Gooseberry Patch

This is delicious served over rice or tossed with noodles!

1 t. soy sauce
2 T. cooking sherry
1/8 t. ground ginger
1/2 t. salt
pepper to taste
1/2 lb. boneless, skinless
    chicken breast, thinly sliced
1/4 c. peanut oil, divided

3 c. snow peas
1/2 c. celery, thinly sliced
5-oz. can sliced bamboo shoots,
    drained
1/2 c. green onions, thinly sliced
1/2 c. sliced mushrooms
1 c. chicken broth

In a bowl, whisk together soy sauce, sherry and seasonings. Add chicken and turn to coat; let marinate 5 minutes. Heat 2 tablespoons oil in a large skillet over high heat. Stirring constantly, cook chicken mixture in oil for 5 minutes, or until cooked through. Remove chicken mixture and keep warm. Add remaining oil to skillet; stir in vegetables and broth. Cook over high heat for 5 minutes, stirring constantly. Add chicken to skillet and cook an additional 5 minutes, stirring constantly. Serves 4 to 6.

Using fresh ginger? Peel it with a spoon rather than a knife.
It's faster and safer plus less will go to waste!

Baked Chicken Burritos

Betsy Johnson
Columbus, OH

Serve with a side of Spanish rice and tortilla chips.

1-1/2 lbs. boneless, skinless
    chicken breasts, chopped
1 c. sour cream
2 c. salsa, divided
2 c. shredded Mexican-blend
    cheese, divided

salt and pepper
8 8-inch flour tortillas
Optional: jalapeño rings
Garnish: sour cream and salsa

Brown chicken in a skillet over medium-high heat until juices run clear when pierced with a fork; drain. Reduce heat to low; stir in sour cream, 1-1/2 cups salsa, 1-1/2 cups cheese, salt and pepper. Stir until cheese melts and completely coats chicken. Divide chicken evenly and spoon into center of tortillas; roll up and place seam-side down in an ungreased 13"x9" baking pan. Spread remaining salsa and cheese over tortillas; sprinkle with jalapeño rings, if desired. Bake, uncovered, at 350 degrees for 25 to 30 minutes. Garnish with sour cream and salsa. Makes 8 servings.

Follow up these quick-as-a-wink burritos with some oh-so-decadent No-Fry Fried Ice Cream...the recipe's on page 203. Festive fare that's easy enough for every day!

Quick as a Wink

Turkey-Bowtie Pasta Salad

*Deidre Sizer
Kettering, OH*

So pretty served cold in half of a cantaloupe.

12-oz. pkg. bowtie pasta
1/2-lb. pkg. cooked turkey
   breast, chopped
1/4 c. green pepper, chopped
1/4 c. red pepper, chopped

1/4 c. onion, minced
2 T. fresh chives, chopped
2 T. fresh parsley, chopped
1-1/4 c. mayonnaise
3 T. honey

Prepare pasta according to package directions; drain. Rinse with cold water; set aside. Combine turkey, peppers, onion, chives and parsley in a large serving bowl; gently fold in pasta. Cover and refrigerate until chilled. In a small bowl, whisk mayonnaise and honey together; pour over salad, stirring until well coated. Serve immediately. Serves 6 to 8.

Line the inside of a cabinet door with self-stick cork tiles to make an oh-so-handy bulletin board. It'll be a great place to tack quick recipes, take-out menus, emergency numbers and more!

Hot Chicken Salad

Delinda Blakney
Scotts Hill, TN

Top with shredded cheese or potato chips
before baking for added flavor.

2 c. cooked chicken, diced
1 c. celery, chopped
1/4 c. slivered almonds
2 to 3 T. lemon juice

1 T. onion, chopped
1/4 c. mayonnaise
10-3/4 oz. can cream of
chicken soup

Combine all ingredients; mix well. Spread into an ungreased
9"x9" baking pan. Bake, uncovered, at 350 degrees for 30 minutes,
or until hot and bubbly. Serves 4.

Chicken Veggie Sandwiches

Kristie Rigo
Friedens, PA

These sandwiches remind me of a chicken fajita.

4 boneless, skinless chicken
breasts, sliced into strips
2 T. oil
1 red pepper, sliced
1 green pepper, sliced
1 sweet onion, thinly sliced

13-1/4 oz. can mushroom stems
and pieces, drained
salt and pepper to taste
1/4 t. red pepper flakes
6 sandwich rolls, split
6 slices provolone cheese

In a skillet over medium heat, cook chicken in oil until juices run clear
when pierced with a fork. Add peppers and onion; sauté until tender.
Stir in mushrooms, salt, pepper and red pepper flakes, heating through.
Spoon warm chicken mixture onto bottom halves of rolls; top with a
slice of cheese and top halves of rolls. Serves 6.

Chicken Salad Croissants
Colleen McAleavey
Pittsburgh, PA

Whether serving for lunch or dinner,
these sandwiches are a winner!

2 to 3 c. cooked chicken, cubed
1/2 c. celery, chopped
1 c. mayonnaise
1/2 c. chopped walnuts
    or pecans

1/2 c. strawberries, hulled
    and sliced
4 to 6 croissants, split

In a bowl, combine all ingredients except croissants; spread evenly on croissant bottom halves. Top with remaining halves. Makes 4 to 6 servings.

Use a drinking straw to hull strawberries with ease. Just push the straw through the end without a stem and the green, leafy top will pop right off!

Stuffed Cranberry Chicken

Meredith Hines
Bennington, VT

Try with other jam combinations for different
tastes...raspberry-orange sounds yummy.

6-oz. pkg. herb-flavored stuffing
   mix
1 lb. boneless, skinless chicken
   breasts
salt and pepper to taste
2 T. olive oil
1/2 c. cranberry-apricot jam
2 T. butter

Prepare stuffing mix as package directs. Flatten chicken breasts between sheets of wax paper; divide and spoon stuffing evenly in the center of each chicken breast. Add salt and pepper to taste. Roll and fold closed; hold together with toothpicks. Heat olive oil in a skillet; brown chicken breasts on both sides. Arrange in an ungreased 1-1/2 quart casserole dish. Bake, uncovered, at 375 degrees for 30 minutes. In a separate pan, heat jam and butter until melted; drizzle over chicken breasts before serving. Makes 2 to 4 servings.

Instead of serving traditional biscuits or dinner rolls with this dish, bake up some sweet and tangy cranberry muffins! Just stir frozen cranberries into cornbread muffin mix and bake as usual.

·*·Quick as a Wink·*·

Easy Chicken Pot Pie

Lynne Gasior
Struthers, OH

Ready-made pie crusts make this homestyle dish extra easy.

2 8-oz. cans chicken, drained
2 13-1/4 oz. cans mixed
   vegetables, drained
2 10-3/4 oz. cans cream of
   chicken soup

1 c. milk
salt and pepper to taste
8-oz. pkg. shredded Cheddar or
   Colby cheese, divided
12-oz. tube refrigerated biscuits

In a bowl, combine all ingredients except cheese and biscuits. Transfer to a greased 13"x9" baking pan; top with 3/4 of cheese. Separate biscuits and tear each into 4 to 5 pieces; place on top of cheese. Sprinkle with remaining cheese. Bake, uncovered, at 350 degrees for 45 minutes, or until biscuits are golden. Serves 4.

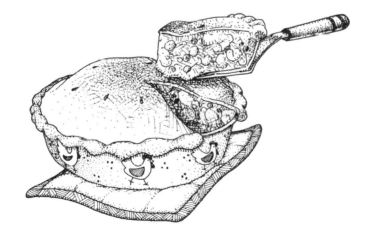

Use a muffin tin in place of individual casseroles when
making mini pot pies, quiche or savory popovers.
So quick & easy!

Crispy Baked Chicken

Vickie
Gooseberry Patch

I needed a creative idea for using up leftover bagel chips...and voilà!
A new twist on bread crumbs.

1 c. mayonnaise
2 cloves garlic, finely chopped
1 T. fresh rosemary, finely
    chopped
2 t. lemon zest
2 T. lemon juice

3/4 c. garlic bagel chips, finely
    crushed
1/4 c. grated Parmesan cheese
4 boneless, skinless chicken
    breasts
2 T. olive oil, divided

In a small bowl, combine mayonnaise, garlic, rosemary and lemon zest. Set aside 1/2 cup of mixture. Stir lemon juice into remaining mixture; cover and refrigerate. Combine crushed bagel chips and Parmesan cheese in a bowl. Arrange chicken in an ungreased 13"x9" baking pan that has been drizzled with one tablespoon olive oil. Brush tops of chicken with reserved mayonnaise mixture. Sprinkle with bread crumb mixture; drizzle with remaining olive oil. Bake, uncovered, at 375 degrees for 25 minutes, or until chicken juices run clear when pierced with a fork. Serve with refrigerated mayonnaise mixture. Makes 4 servings.

Kids love Crispy Baked Chicken...especially when it's followed by dessert! Make up some bite-size ice cream treats by sandwiching fruity sherbet between vanilla wafers.

Quick as a Wink

Potato-Chicken Bake

Coleen Lambert
Casco, WI

Just as good the next day, so be sure to make twice as much.

3 c. potatoes, peeled, boiled and
    mashed
1 c. shredded Cheddar cheese,
    divided
6-oz. can French fried onions,
    divided
1-1/2 c. cooked chicken, cubed
10-oz. pkg. frozen mixed
    vegetables, thawed

10-3/4 oz. can cream of
    chicken soup
1/4 c. milk
1/4 t. pepper
1/2 t. dry mustard
1/4 t. garlic powder

Combine potatoes, 1/2 cup cheese and 1/2 can onions; mix well.
Spread in a greased 2-quart casserole dish; set aside. Mix chicken,
vegetables, soup, milk and seasonings together; spread over potato
mixture. Bake, uncovered, at 375 degrees for 30 minutes; top with
remaining cheese and onions. Return to oven until cheese melts, 3 to
5 minutes. Makes 4 to 6 servings.

French fried onions give a flavor punch to any dish...try
them mixed in meatloaf, stirred into stuffing or
to top mashed potatoes.

Hot Turkey Casserole

Kelley Nicholson
Gooseberry Patch

This tasty dish is a great way to use up leftover Thanksgiving turkey. It also makes a good sandwich filling!

2 c. cooked turkey, cubed
2 c. celery, chopped
2 t. onion, grated
1/2 c. chopped pecans
1/2 t. salt

1 c. low-fat plain yogurt
2 T. lemon juice
1/2 c. shredded Cheddar cheese
1 c. potato chips, crushed

In a bowl, mix together turkey, celery, onion, pecans and salt. Stir in yogurt and lemon juice until evenly blended. Spoon into a greased 13"x9" baking pan. Sprinkle with cheese and potato chips. Bake, uncovered, at 450 degrees for 15 minutes, or until cheese melts. Serves 4.

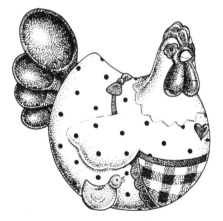

Make crescent rolls extra special for every day...before rolling them up, sprinkle on some Monterey Jack cheese and add a teaspoon of salsa. Zesty and oh-so delicious!

Coffee-Braised Chicken

Clarene Ho
Incline Village, NV

A family favorite especially when served with steamed white rice and garnished with green onions and chopped cilantro.

5 lbs. boneless, skinless chicken, cubed
2/3 c. soy sauce
1/3 c. coffee
1 c. sugar

1 c. water
1 t. fresh ginger, peeled and minced
2 cloves garlic, minced

Add all ingredients to a large stockpot; bring to a boil. Reduce heat; cover and simmer over medium heat for 30 to 40 minutes without stirring or uncovering. Shake stockpot once or twice during cooking. Serves 6.

Next-Day Chicken Bake

Lucille Dahlberg
Glendale, CA

Great for ladies' luncheons alongside fruit salad and some freshly baked muffins.

1 c. cooked chicken, diced
1 c. cooked rice
1/4 c. almonds, toasted and chopped
1 green onion, chopped
10-3/4 oz. can cream of mushroom soup

1/2 t. salt
1 to 2 t. lemon juice
1/2 c. mayonnaise
3/4 c. celery, chopped
2 to 3 eggs, hard-boiled, peeled and chopped
1 c. potato chips, crumbled

Combine all ingredients except potato chips in an ungreased 2-quart casserole dish; cover and refrigerate overnight. Bring to room temperature; sprinkle with potato chips. Bake, uncovered, at 375 degrees for 30 to 45 minutes. Serves 4.

Alfredo Pasta with Chicken
Sherrie Sheetz
Camp Hill, PA

Rich and creamy...you won't believe how easy this dish can be.

16-oz. pkg. penne pasta
2 boneless, skinless chicken
    breasts, cubed
2-1/2 c. whipping cream
1 c. butter

1 egg, beaten
1 c. grated Parmesan cheese
salt and pepper to taste
2 c. frozen green beans, thawed
2 c. frozen carrots, thawed

Prepare pasta according to package directions; drain. Sauté chicken in a skillet over medium-high heat until juices run clear when pierced with a fork; set aside. Warm cream, butter and egg in a saucepan over low heat until butter melts; do not boil. Add Parmesan cheese, salt and pepper; whisk until blended. Combine pasta, chicken, vegetables and cream mixture; warm through. Makes 8 to 10 servings.

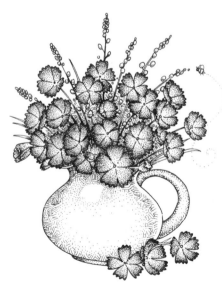

Don„t forget about prepared Alfredo sauce in a jar when time is really short! Mix cooked chicken, pasta and veggies together in a saucepan and top it off with ready-made sauce...heat through and dinner's done.

Turkey Tortilla Soup

Angie Venable
Ostrander, OH

This super-simple meal takes only 20 minutes from start to finish!

1 c. salsa
2 14-oz. cans chicken broth
2 c. cooked turkey, cubed
1 zucchini, coarsely chopped

Garnish: sour cream, shredded
   cheese, diced avocado,
   crushed tortilla chips

In a large saucepan, combine salsa and broth; bring to a boil over medium-high heat. Add turkey and zucchini; cook until zucchini is tender. Serve in bowls, garnished as desired. Makes 4 servings.

Serve up soup in mugs topped with homemade herbed croutons. Cut out fun shapes from sliced bread, brush with butter, sprinkle with herbs and bake at 200 degrees until golden and crisp.

Chicken-Apple Skillet

Kimberly Burns
Wanamassa, NJ

Sprinkle crystallized ginger on top.

8-oz. pkg. fine egg noodles
3 lbs. boneless, skinless chicken
   breasts, chopped
2 T. oil
1 onion, chopped
1 clove garlic, minced
1/4 c. chicken broth
1 c. apple juice

1 T. fresh ginger, peeled
   and minced
1 c. plain yogurt
1 T. cornstarch
2 apples, cored, peeled
   and chopped
pepper to taste

Prepare noodles according to package directions; drain and keep warm. In a skillet, sauté chicken in oil until juices run clear when pierced with a fork; remove to a platter. Sauté onion and garlic in same skillet until tender; add broth, apple juice and ginger. Cook over medium heat until liquid is reduced to about one cup. Stir yogurt and cornstarch together in a small bowl; add to skillet. Mix in apples and chicken; season with pepper. Reduce heat; simmer for 5 minutes. Spoon over warm noodles to serve. Serves 4.

Plain yogurt is a great healthy substitution for sour cream. For a scrumptious pasta salad, toss cooked pasta, fresh veggies and yogurt flavored with Dijon mustard. Add chicken, turkey or tuna to create a hearty main dish.

Quick as a Wink

Chicken & Cranberry Pasta *Barbie Harmon*
Phoenix, AZ

Start a new Thanksgiving tradition with this simple dish.

1 c. sweetened, dried cranberries
1/3 c. cranberry juice cocktail
1/2 c. green onions, chopped
2 T. butter
1/2 c. all-purpose flour
1 t. paprika
1 t. dried thyme

1/2 t. salt
pepper to taste
1-1/2 lbs. boneless, skinless
    chicken breasts, thinly sliced
16-oz. can chicken broth
12-oz. pkg. bowtie pasta, cooked

Combine cranberries and juice in a microwave-safe bowl; microwave on high setting for one minute and set aside. In a skillet over medium heat, sauté onions in butter for 5 minutes; set aside. Mix flour, paprika, thyme, salt and pepper in a plastic zipping bag; add chicken, shaking to coat. Sauté chicken in skillet for 5 minutes; add onions and chicken broth. Simmer 5 to 6 minutes. Drain cranberries; stir into chicken mixture, heating through. Fold in pasta; toss gently. Makes 4 to 6 servings.

Having steamed veggies on the side? Serve them up in individual ramekins or, if serving fresh veggies, use paper muffin cups for a special touch.

Gobbler Cobbler

Sandy Rowe
Bellevue, OH

No leftover turkey on hand? Use chicken instead.

2-1/2 c. turkey gravy
3 c. cooked turkey, cubed
1-1/2 c. frozen peas, partially
   thawed
1-1/2 c. sliced mushrooms
2/3 c. sun-dried tomatoes,
   chopped
1/4 c. water

2 T. fresh parsley, chopped
   and divided
1 t. poultry seasoning, divided
2-1/4 c. buttermilk biscuit
   baking mix
1/4 t. pepper
3/4 c. plus 2 T. milk

Combine gravy, turkey, peas, mushrooms, tomatoes, water, one tablespoon parsley and 1/2 teaspoon poultry seasoning in a large stockpot. Stir occasionally over medium heat until mixture comes to a boil. In another bowl, combine baking mix, remaining parsley, remaining poultry seasoning, pepper and milk; mix well. Pour turkey mixture into an ungreased 2-quart casserole dish; drop biscuit mixture on top in 6 equal mounds. Place on a baking sheet; bake, uncovered, at 450 degrees for 20 minutes, or until topping is golden. Serves 6.

No poultry seasoning in the cupboard? Combine
1/4 teaspoon each of dried parsley, sage, rosemary,
marjoram and pepper. Store remaining
mixture in an airtight container.

Baby Hot Browns

JoAnn
Gooseberry Patch

*If you're planning a party, you can't go wrong with
these wonderful crowd-pleasing appetizers.*

24 party pumpernickel bread
    slices
3 T. butter
3 T. all-purpose flour
1 c. milk
1-1/2 c. shredded sharp Cheddar
    cheese
1-1/2 c. cooked turkey, diced

1/4 t. salt
1/4 t. cayenne pepper
1/2 c. shredded Parmesan
    cheese
6 bacon slices, crisply cooked,
    crumbled and divided
5 plum tomatoes, thinly sliced

Arrange bread slices on lightly greased baking sheets. Broil 3 to
4 minutes, until toasted. Melt butter in a saucepan over medium heat,
whisking in flour until smooth. Whisk in milk and cook until
thickened, stirring constantly. Add Cheddar cheese, whisking until
melted. Stir in turkey, salt and cayenne pepper. Top bread slices evenly
with mixture. Sprinkle with Parmesan cheese and half of bacon. Bake
at 500 degrees for 2 minutes, or until Parmesan is melted. Top with
tomato slices and sprinkle with remaining bacon. Makes 2 dozen.

Before chopping nuts in
a food processor, dust
them with flour
or powdered
sugar...they'll chop
easily and won't stick
to the blades!

Oniony Chicken Casserole
Holly Sutton
Middleburgh, NY

No chicken on hand? Use pork chops instead!

10-3/4 oz. can cream of
  mushroom soup
10-3/4 oz. can cream of
  celery soup
1 c. milk
1 c. instant rice, uncooked

2 to 3 lbs. boneless, skinless
  chicken breasts or thighs
1-1/2 oz. pkg. onion soup mix
1 t. garlic, minced
1 t. onion salt

Mix soups, milk and rice together; spread in a greased 13"x9" baking pan. Arrange chicken over the top; sprinkle with onion soup mix, garlic and onion salt. Bake, covered, at 350 degrees for 45 to 50 minutes, or until chicken juices run clear. Makes 6 servings.

Freezing cooked rice makes for quick-fix meals later.
Use it for stir-fry dishes, to make soups thick and hearty,
or mix in fresh vegetables for an easy side dish…just freeze
servings flat in plastic zipping bags. How clever!

Quick as a Wink

Citrus Chicken with Rice

Joyce Crider
Landisville, PA

Serve on toast, croissants or a bed of lettuce...make two or three times the amount for a shower luncheon.

2 T. oil
3 boneless, skinless chicken
   breasts, chopped
1/2 c. mayonnaise-type salad
   dressing
1/2 c. orange juice
2 T. brown sugar, packed

1 c. cooked rice
1 green pepper, sliced
11-oz. can mandarin oranges,
   drained
8-oz. can pineapple chunks,
   drained

Heat oil in a skillet over medium-high heat; add chicken. Sauté until juices run clear when pierced with a fork, about 3 minutes; drain. Reduce heat to medium; stir in salad dressing, juice and brown sugar. Add rice and green pepper; bring to a boil. Remove from heat; fold in oranges and pineapple. Let stand, covered, for 5 minutes before serving. Makes 4 servings.

Freeze peach and nectarine slices and keep on hand for adding to milkshakes, ice cream, fruity punches or just to nibble.

Lunch on the porch

Creamy Turkey Lasagna

Jennifer Stout
Blandon, PA

A family favorite...once you taste it, you'll make it all the time.

8-oz. pkg. lasagna noodles
10-3/4 oz. can cream of
  mushroom soup
10-3/4 oz. can cream of
  chicken soup
1 c. grated Parmesan cheese

1 c. sour cream
1/4 c. chopped pimentos
2 to 3 c. cooked turkey, chopped
1 c. onion, chopped
1/2 t. garlic salt
2 c. shredded Cheddar cheese

Prepare noodles according to package directions; drain. Combine all ingredients except lasagna noodles and Cheddar cheese. Spread 1/4 of the turkey mixture in an ungreased 13"x9" baking pan; place some noodles on top. Alternate layers of turkey and noodles. Sprinkle with cheese; bake, uncovered, at 350 degrees for 40 to 45 minutes. Let stand 10 minutes before serving. Serves 8.

Make this lasagna the night before and store in the fridge for an even speedier dinner. Just add 10 minutes to the baking time...so easy!

Treats
in a
Twinkle

Double Delight Cookies

DeeAnn Portra
Turtle Lake, ND

*We often double the recipe and use an ice cream scoop
for the dough...extra large and extra good!*

1 c. butter-flavored shortening
3/4 c. sugar
1/2 c. brown sugar, packed
2 eggs, beaten
2 T. milk
1 t. vanilla extract
2 T. baking cocoa

2-1/3 c. all-purpose flour
1 t. baking soda
1/2 t. salt
1 c. chopped pecans
1 c. semi-sweet chocolate
   chunks

In a large bowl, beat shortening and sugars; blend in eggs, milk and
vanilla. In another bowl, combine remaining ingredients except pecans
and chocolate chunks; add to shortening mixture, blending well. Fold
in pecans and chocolate chunks. Drop by rounded tablespoonfuls
2 inches apart on ungreased baking sheets; bake at 375 degrees for
10 to 12 minutes. Cool on wire racks. Makes 6 dozen.

Lunch in a flash! Pack small plastic zipping bags with a few
cookies each...place all the little bags into one big freezer
bag. Freeze and use for lunches as needed!

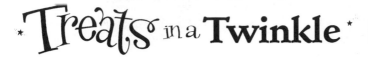

Treats in a Twinkle

Night & Day Cookies

Elisabeth Macmillan
British Columbia, Canada

With both white and dark chocolate, they look like night and day but they're also good enough to eat all night and day!

1 c. butter, softened
1 c. brown sugar, packed
1 c. sugar
2 t. vanilla extract
2/3 c. baking cocoa

2 eggs, beaten
1 t. baking soda
2 c. all-purpose flour
2 c. white chocolate chips
2 c. semi-sweet chocolate chips

In a bowl, beat butter, sugars and vanilla until fluffy; blend in cocoa, eggs and baking soda. Add flour; mix well. Fold in chips; shape dough into 1-1/2 inch balls. Place 3 inches apart on greased baking sheets; bake at 325 degrees for 14 to 16 minutes. Cool on baking sheets for 2 minutes; transfer to wire racks. Makes about 4 dozen.

Sue's Cut-Out Cookies

Sue Green
Corona, CA

These cookies hold their shape well when baked. They may also be rolled out very thick for making "cookie pops."

1 c. butter-flavored shortening
3/4 c. sugar
3-oz. pkg. cream cheese,
    softened

1 egg, beaten
1/2 t. vanilla extract
2 c. all-purpose flour
16-oz. container frosting

In a bowl, beat shortening, sugar, cream cheese, egg and vanilla. Add flour, mixing well. Roll out on a lightly floured surface to 1/4-inch thickness; cut into desired shapes using cookie cutters. Place on ungreased baking sheets. Bake at 325 degrees until golden, about 15 to 20 minutes. Cool and frost. Makes about 2 dozen.

Cocoa Streusel Bars

Kris Warner
Circleville, OH

Who cares what's for dinner…let's go straight to dessert!

1-3/4 c. all-purpose flour
1-1/2 c. powdered sugar
1/2 c. baking cocoa
1 c. butter
8-oz. pkg. cream cheese,
    softened

14-oz. can sweetened condensed
    milk
1 egg, beaten
2 t. vanilla extract

In a bowl, combine flour, sugar and cocoa; cut in butter until coarse crumbs form. Reserve 2 cups of flour mixture; press remaining flour mixture into an ungreased 13"x9" glass baking pan. Bake at 350 degrees for 15 minutes; set aside. In a separate bowl, beat cream cheese until fluffy; add milk, egg and vanilla, mixing well. Spoon over crust; sprinkle with reserved flour mixture. Bake, uncovered, at 350 degrees for 25 minutes; cool to room temperature and then refrigerate until firm. Cut into bars to serve. Makes 20.

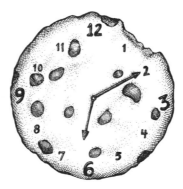

Make s'mores even easier! Use striped fudge cookies
instead of graham crackers and sandwich a
marshmallow between them. Just microwave
and they're ready in a flash.

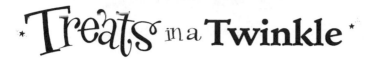

Pecan Chippers

Julie Anderson
Joliet, IL

The 3 C's...crunchy, chocolatey and chock-full of goodness.

1-1/2 c. whole-wheat flour
3/4 c. all-purpose flour
1 t. baking soda
1/4 t. salt
1 c. butter
1 c. light brown sugar, packed

1/2 c. dark brown sugar, packed
2 eggs, beaten
2 t. vanilla extract
1-1/2 c. white chocolate chips
3/4 c. chopped pecans

In a bowl, combine flours, baking soda and salt; set aside. In a separate large bowl, beat butter and sugars; blend in eggs and vanilla. Add flour mixture until just combined; fold in chocolate chips and pecans. Drop by rounded tablespoonfuls onto ungreased baking sheets; bake at 325 degrees for 13 to 15 minutes. Makes about 5 dozen.

Punch in a Pinch

Kathy Riggs
Lewiston, ID

Need a quick drink for snack night and out of juice boxes? Add ice to a thermos jug and fill with juices, adding ginger ale at the last minute...don't forget the cups!

2 c. orange juice
1 c. lemon juice

1 c. grenadine
2 qts. ginger ale, chilled

Stir juices and grenadine together in a serving bowl; chill. Add ginger ale right before serving. Makes 24 servings.

Peanut Butter Power Squares

Leigh Pickens
Round Rock, TX

Healthy and packed with flavor.

1/2 c. honey
1/2 c. brown sugar, packed
1 c. crunchy peanut butter

4 c. whole-grain rice flake cereal
1 c. dried fruit bits

Bring honey and brown sugar to a boil in a heavy saucepan; remove from heat. Mix in peanut butter; stir until melted. Fold in cereal and fruit bits; press mixture into an ungreased 11"x9" baking pan. Cut into squares with a pizza cutter while still warm; cool. Makes one dozen.

Cinnamon Sticks

Barbara Panitzke
Redwood Falls, MN

These remind me of baked pie dough sparkling
with cinnamon & sugar.

1/2 c. shortening
1/2 c. butter
3/4 c. plus 1 T. sugar, divided
2 c. all-purpose flour

1/2 t. salt
1/2 t. vanilla extract
1 T. almond extract
1 t. cinnamon

In a bowl, combine shortening, butter, 5 tablespoons sugar, flour, salt and extracts; mix well. Roll dough out on a lightly floured surface to 1/2-inch thickness; slice into 2-inch by 1/2-inch strips. Arrange on ungreased baking sheets; bake at 375 degrees for 12 minutes, or until golden. Toss remaining sugar and cinnamon together in a pie pan; roll hot sticks in mixture until well coated. Makes 3 to 4 dozen.

Cinnamon Gingersnaps

Lisa Ashton
Aston, PA

*These spicy-sweet cookies are so nice for dipping into a cup
of hot coffee or herbal tea.*

3/4 c. butter, softened
1 c. brown sugar, packed
1 egg, beaten
1/4 c. molasses
2-1/4 c. all-purpose flour

2 t. baking soda
1/2 t. salt
2 t. cinnamon
1 t. ground ginger
1/2 to 1 c. sugar

Blend together butter and brown sugar in a large bowl. Stir in egg and
molasses; set aside. In a separate bowl, combine flour, baking soda,
salt and spices. Gradually add flour mixture to butter mixture; mix
well. Roll dough into one-inch balls; roll in sugar. Arrange on
ungreased baking sheets, 2 inches apart. Bake at 350 degrees for 10 to
12 minutes, until cookies are set and tops are cracked. Remove to wire
racks; cool completely. Makes 4 dozen.

Spread cool and creamy vanilla ice cream between
Gingersnaps and freeze...a yummy way to finish off
a delicious dinner of Chicken Stir-Fry. Find the
recipe on page 169.

Especially Good Brownies

Carol Knebel
Antioch, CA

For out-of-this-world richness, ice with fudgy frosting when cooled.

2 c. sugar
4 eggs, beaten
4 1-oz. sqs. unsweetened
   baking chocolate

1 c. unsalted butter
2 t. vanilla extract
1 c. all-purpose flour
2 c. chopped pecans

In a bowl, beat sugar and eggs for one minute; set aside. Melt chocolate and butter in a double boiler, stirring until smooth; let cool to room temperature. Stir into sugar mixture until just blended; add vanilla. Mix in flour and pecans until just blended; spread into an ungreased 13"x9" baking pan. Bake at 350 degrees for 30 minutes; cool and cut into squares. Makes 12 to 15.

Make a pudding shake! Combine 1-1/2 cups milk
with 1/2 cup ready-made pudding...blend and
pour for a creamy treat.

Butterscotch Brownies

Alice Flood
Dallas, TX

This is my favorite recipe...the brown sugar gives the brownies an extra-rich butterscotch flavor.

1/4 c. butter	1 t. baking powder
1 c. brown sugar, packed	1/2 t. salt
1 egg, beaten	1/2 t. vanilla extract
3/4 c. all-purpose flour	1/2 c. chopped nuts

Melt butter in a small saucepan over low heat; remove from heat. Stir in brown sugar until dissolved; set aside to cool to room temperature. Blend in egg; add flour, baking powder and salt, mixing well. Stir in vanilla and nuts; spread in a greased 8"x8" baking pan. Bake at 350 degrees for 25 minutes; let cool. Makes 9.

Need a little something extra on cakes and brownies? Try topping with chopped candy bars! Make chopping a breeze when you wrap them in plastic and freeze for 10 to 15 minutes beforehand.

Peanut Butter Pan Cake

Molly Maysilles
Lancaster, PA

A tall glass of icy cold milk is all that's missing.

3 c. all-purpose flour
2 c. sugar
2 t. baking soda
1 t. salt
1/4 c. baking cocoa

2 t. vanilla extract
3/4 c. oil
2 T. vinegar
2 c. water

Combine flour, sugar, baking soda, salt and baking cocoa in a large bowl; mix well. Add vanilla, oil and vinegar; stir in water, mixing well. Spread into a lightly greased 13"x9" baking pan; bake at 350 degrees for 35 minutes. Spread Peanut Butter Frosting on cake when cool. Makes 15 servings.

Peanut Butter Frosting:

2 c. powdered sugar
1 c. shortening
1-1/2 t. vanilla extract

1/2 to 3/4 c. milk
1 c. creamy peanut butter

Combine sugar, shortening and vanilla until smooth and creamy, adding enough milk to reach desired spreading consistency. Stir in peanut butter; mix well.

Anchor layer cakes to serving pedestals with a dab of frosting before starting to decorate. The cake will stay in place, making frosting and decorating lots easier!

Triple Fudge Cake

Tanya Leach
Adamstown, PA

I get requests for this cake all the time and nothing could be easier!

3.4-oz. pkg. cook & serve
   chocolate pudding mix
18-1/2 oz. pkg. chocolate cake
   mix

12-oz. pkg. semi-sweet
   chocolate chips
Optional: vanilla ice cream

Prepare pudding according to package directions; stir in cake mix.
Spread in a greased 13"x9" baking pan; sprinkle with chocolate chips.
Bake at 350 degrees for 35 minutes; cool. Serve with vanilla ice cream,
if desired. Makes 12 servings.

Cake stuck to the bottom of the pan? Dip the bottom
of the pan in hot water and it'll pop right out!

Butterscotch Cheesecake Bars

Marsha Konken
Sterling, CO

*A bake-sale favorite! Cut into small squares and set each in a
frilled cupcake paper for a pretty presentation.*

6-oz. pkg. butterscotch chips
1/3 c. butter
2 c. graham cracker crumbs
1 c. chopped pecans
8-oz. pkg. cream
    cheese, softened

14-oz. can sweetened condensed
    milk
1 t. vanilla extract
1 egg, beaten

Melt butterscotch chips and butter in a saucepan over medium-low
heat; stir in cracker crumbs and pecans. Press half of mixture into an
ungreased 13"x9" baking pan. Beat cream cheese in a large bowl until
fluffy; stir in condensed milk. Add vanilla and egg; mix well and pour
over crumb mixture. Top with remaining crumb mixture. Bake at
350 degrees for 25 to 30 minutes. Chill until firm; cut into bars.
Makes about 1-1/2 dozen.

Apricot Balls

Kaki Huckstep
Kingsport, TN

*This recipe came from Grandma. My mom, sister and I bake them
every year...wonderful and so easy.*

2/3 c. sweetened condensed
    milk
2 c. flaked coconut

1 c. dried apricots, chopped
1/8 t. salt

Combine all ingredients in a large bowl; mix well. Shape into
one-inch balls; place on a lightly greased baking sheet. Bake at
350 degrees until golden, about 12 to 15 minutes. Makes 2 dozen.

Treats in a Twinkle

Cherry-Almond Bars

Deb DeYoung
Zeeland, MI

Make ahead of time...these bars freeze well.

1 c. shortening
2 c. sugar
4 eggs, beaten
1 t. vanilla extract

1 t. almond extract
3 c. all-purpose flour
1 t. salt
14-1/2 oz. can cherry pie filling

In a bowl, beat shortening and sugar. Add eggs, extracts, flour and salt; mix well. Spread 3/4 of batter in a greased 15"x10" jelly-roll pan; spread pie filling over the top. Dot with remaining batter; bake at 350 degrees for 30 to 35 minutes, until golden. Drizzle with Almond Glaze while still warm; cut into bars to serve. Makes about 3 dozen.

Almond Glaze:

1 c. powdered sugar
1/2 t. vanilla extract

1/2 t. almond extract
2 to 3 T. milk

Stir all ingredients together until creamy.

Vanilla pudding makes a quick topper for fresh berries...add whipped topping for an extra-fluffy vanilla mousse. Try it with pound cake and shortcake too!

Fudgy No-Bake Cookies

Shirley Pritchett
Pinckneyville, IL

*Add a cupful of nuts in place of, or right along
with, the coconut for added crunch.*

1-1/2 c. sugar
1/2 c. baking cocoa
1/2 c. milk
1/2 c. margarine

1 t. vanilla extract
3 c. quick-cooking oats,
   uncooked
1 c. flaked coconut

Bring sugar, baking cocoa, milk and margarine to a rolling boil in a
heavy saucepan over high heat. Remove from heat and stir in vanilla,
oats and coconut. Drop by teaspoonfuls onto wax paper; let cool until
firm. Makes about 4 dozen.

Chocolate dessert cups are easy to make. Just paint
paper muffin cups with melted chocolate, chill until firm
and peel off the paper. Serve on a chilled plate so that
the cups will keep their shape.

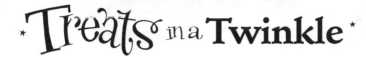

No-Fry Fried Ice Cream

Renee Lewis
Basin, WY

A quick & easy shortcut to a Mexican favorite.

4 c. honey-coated corn flake
   cereal, crushed
2 T. sugar
2 T. margarine, melted
1/4 c. corn syrup

2 T. cinnamon
1 gal. vanilla ice cream, softened
Garnish: chocolate syrup and
   frozen whipped topping,
   thawed

In a large bowl, toss corn flake cereal with sugar, margarine, corn syrup and cinnamon; set aside. Scoop ice cream into 3-inch balls; roll in cereal mixture, pressing mixture lightly to coat ball. Place ice cream balls in muffin tins; freeze until ready to serve. To serve, place ice cream ball on a serving plate, add a dollop of whipped topping and drizzle with chocolate syrup. Makes about 8.

Make a scrumptious sauce for pound cake or ice cream.
Purée fruit preserves with a few tablespoons of
fruit juice…yummy!

Go-Bananas Coffee Cake

Sandy Bernards
Valencia, CA

A yummy treat for breakfast or anytime!

8-oz. pkg. cream cheese,
   softened
1/2 c. butter, softened
1-1/4 c. sugar
2 eggs

3 bananas, mashed
1 t. vanilla extract
2-1/4 c. all-purpose flour
1-1/2 t. baking powder
1/2 t. baking soda

In a large bowl with an electric blender on medium speed, blend cream cheese, butter and sugar until fluffy. Add eggs, one at a time, blending well after each addition. Mix in bananas and vanilla; set aside. In a separate bowl, combine flour, baking powder and baking soda; gradually add to cream cheese mixture, mixing well. Stir in half the Pecan Topping; pour into a greased 13"x9" baking pan. Sprinkle with remaining Pecan Topping; bake at 350 degrees for 25 to 30 minutes. Serves 12.

Pecan Topping:

1 c. chopped pecans
2 T. sugar

1 t. cinnamon

Toss ingredients together until pecans are well coated.

Use a pastry blender
to slice or mash
bananas to desired
consistency...so
quick & easy!

Best-Ever Cupcakes

Molly Myers
Millheim, PA

Easy to pack for treat nights...be it Scouts, soccer, swim team or a classroom celebration. Just frost and decorate accordingly!

1-1/2 c. all-purpose flour
3 T. baking cocoa
1 c. sugar
1 t. baking soda
1/2 t. salt

6 T. oil
1 t. vanilla extract
1 c. cold water
16-oz. container frosting

In a bowl, blend all ingredients except frosting; fill 12 paper-lined muffin cups 2/3 full. Bake at 350 degrees for 20 minutes; cool before frosting. Makes one dozen.

Homemade Lemonade Syrup

Sheila Holland
Corydon, KY

So easy to make...a real time-saver to have on hand.

2 c. sugar
1 c. water

1 c. lemon juice

Bring sugar and water to a boil in a small saucepan over high heat; boil for 5 minutes, stirring occasionally. Remove from heat; stir in lemon juice. Set aside to cool; cover and refrigerate. To serve, stir 2 tablespoons syrup into 3/4 cup cold water; add ice. Makes 20 servings.

Make ghastly good cupcakes for Halloween! Bake chocolate cupcakes and add shoestring licorice pieces for legs and two chocolate chip eyes. Spooky chocolate spiders...kids love 'em!

Lemon Pastries

Carol Hickman
Kingsport, TN

*Fancy made simple...sprinkle with powdered sugar and add a curl
or two of lemon zest right before serving.*

8-oz. pkg. cream cheese,
   softened
1/2 c. sugar

1 T. lemon juice
2 8-oz. tubes refrigerated
   crescent rolls

In a bowl, blend cream cheese, sugar and lemon juice; set aside. Unroll
crescent rolls and divide along perforations into triangles; spread with
cream cheese mixture. Roll up crescent roll-style; bake on ungreased
baking sheets at 350 degrees for 20 minutes. Let cool; spoon Glaze
over the tops before serving. Makes 16.

Glaze:

1/2 c. powdered sugar
1 t. vanilla extract

1 to 2 T. milk

Whisk ingredients together until smooth and creamy.

Making Lemon Pastries
for a crowd? Cut the
crescent roll triangles in
half, fill with half the
filling and make twice as
many minis!

Treats in a Twinkle

Batch for a Bunch Cookies

Terri Childress
Staunton, VA

*A class of 22, a team of 12...the number of cookies needed
determines their size!*

1/2 c. sugar
1/2 c. brown sugar, packed
1/3 c. margarine, softened
1/3 c. shortening
1 egg, beaten
1-1/2 t. vanilla extract

1/2 t. baking soda
1/2 t. salt
1-1/2 c. all-purpose flour
1/2 c. chopped nuts
1 c. semi-sweet chocolate chips

In a bowl, blend sugars, margarine, shortening, egg, vanilla, baking soda and salt together; blend in flour until just mixed. Fold in nuts and chocolate chips; drop by spoonfuls onto ungreased baking sheets. Bake at 375 degrees for 12 to 13 minutes. Makes 2 to 3 dozen.

Making drop cookies on a lazy Sunday afternoon?
Double the batch and only bake half. Roll the rest
into balls and freeze them on a cookie sheet, then
transfer to a plastic zipping bag. Ready-to-bake
cookies whenever you need them!

Ooey-Gooey Butter Cake

Gayla Weltzer
Camden, OH

Yum says it all!

18-1/2 oz. pkg. yellow cake mix
4 eggs, divided
1/2 c. butter, softened

16-oz. pkg. powdered sugar
8-oz. pkg. cream cheese,
   softened

In a bowl, combine dry cake mix, 2 eggs and butter; spread into a greased 13"x9" baking pan. In a separate bowl, combine powdered sugar, cream cheese and remaining eggs; blend well. Spread over cake mixture; bake at 375 degrees for 40 to 45 minutes. Cool; cut into squares to serve. Makes 24 servings.

Butterscotch Cake

Phyllis Peters
Three Rivers, MI

My cousin Edward shared this simple recipe with me.

18-1/2 oz. pkg. yellow cake mix
15-3/4 oz. can butterscotch
   pie filling

3 eggs, beaten
12-oz. pkg. butterscotch chips

In a bowl, combine dry cake mix, pie filling and eggs; spread in a greased 13"x9" baking pan. Sprinkle with butterscotch chips. Bake at 350 degrees for 35 to 40 minutes or until a toothpick inserted in the center removes clean. Serves 12.

This quick & easy Butterscotch Cake will taste just right after a hearty dinner of Brown Sugar Ham Roll-Ups. Pair them with the recipe on page 121.

Dump-It Cake

Kristy Gatz
Wichita, KS

With only one pan to clean, this cake is sure to become every mom's favorite.

20-oz. can crushed pineapple
21-oz. can cherry pie filling
18-1/2 oz. pkg. yellow cake mix

1/2 to 1 c. chopped pecans
3/4 c. butter, sliced

Spread pineapple with juice in an ungreased 13"x9" baking pan; gently spoon cherry pie filling on top. Sprinkle dry cake mix over top; do not stir. Arrange pecans on top; dot with butter. Bake at 350 degrees for 50 to 55 minutes. Makes 12 servings.

Slice of Sunshine Cake

Michelle Campen
Peoria, IL

This sweet treat is so quick & easy to mix up right from the pantry!

18-1/2 oz. pkg. yellow cake mix
1/4 c. applesauce
4 eggs, beaten
11-oz. can mandarin oranges, undrained
8-oz. container frozen whipped topping, thawed

3.4-oz. pkg. instant vanilla pudding mix
15-1/2 oz. can crushed pineapple, drained

In a bowl, combine dry cake mix, applesauce, eggs and oranges; mix well. Pour into a lightly greased 13"x9" baking pan. Bake at 350 degrees for 30 to 40 minutes or until a toothpick inserted in the center removes clean; set aside to cool completely. Blend remaining ingredients together; spread over cake. Refrigerate until serving. Serves 16.

Caramel Layer Brownies

Lisa Brossmann
Milwaukee, WI

Cake mix makes these the easiest homemade brownies yet.

14-oz. pkg. caramels,
   unwrapped
2/3 c. evaporated milk, divided
18-1/2 oz. pkg. German
   chocolate cake mix

3/4 c. butter, melted
1 c. chopped nuts
1 c. semi-sweet chocolate chips

In a heavy saucepan over medium heat, stir together caramels and 1/3 cup evaporated milk. Mix until melted and smooth; set aside. Combine dry cake mix, butter, remaining evaporated milk and nuts; mix just until moistened. Press half of cake mixture into the bottom of a 13"x9" baking pan that has been sprayed with non-stick vegetable spray; bake at 350 degrees for 6 minutes. Sprinkle with chocolate chips; spread caramel mixture over the top. Flatten pieces of remaining cake mixture with your hands and place over the caramel layer; bake for 15 to 18 minutes. Cool slightly; refrigerate for 30 minutes, or until caramel layer becomes firm. Cut into bars to serve. Makes 3 dozen.

In a 8"x8" baking pan, combine a 14-ounce bag of
caramels with a 5-ounce can of evaporated milk,
1/2 cup chocolate chips and 1/2 teaspoon vanilla. Bake
at 350 degrees for 30 minutes until melted and smooth.
Dip fresh fruit and enjoy!

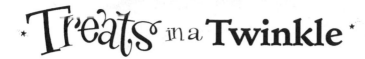

Chocolate Éclair Squares

Vickie Haley
Corona, CA

Pop 'em in the freezer to chill quicker!

14.4-oz. box graham crackers
3.9-oz. pkg. instant chocolate
   pudding mix
2 c. plus 3 T. milk, divided
8-oz. container frozen whipped
   topping, thawed and divided

3.4-oz. pkg. instant vanilla
   pudding mix
2 1-oz. sqs. unsweetened
   baking chocolate, melted
6 T. margarine, melted
1-1/2 c. powdered sugar

Line the bottom of an ungreased 13"x9" baking pan with a single layer of graham crackers; set aside. In a bowl, combine dry chocolate pudding mix with one cup milk; fold in half the whipped topping. Spread over graham crackers; add another layer of graham crackers on top. Repeat process using vanilla pudding; top with graham crackers. Blend remaining ingredients; pour over the top. Refrigerate overnight. Serves 10 to 12.

Keep a small, new powder puff in the powdered sugar canister and use it to dust cake pans and rolling surfaces. Extra sweet and extra easy!

Quick Cherry Dessert

Sharon Boling
Bristow, VA

No pie filling on hand? Try it with frozen berries instead.

18-1/2 oz. pkg. white cake mix
1/2 c. butter

2 21-oz. cans cherry pie filling
Optional: whipped topping

Pour dry cake mix into a bowl; cut in butter with a pastry cutter or fork until mixture resembles coarse crumbs. Set aside. Spread pie filling in a lightly greased 13"x9" baking pan; spoon cake mixture evenly over the top. Bake at 350 degrees until golden and bubbly, about 35 to 45 minutes. Serve with whipped topping, if desired. Makes 15 to 18 servings.

Strawberry Angel Bites

Sandy Poos
Highland, IL

So pretty in sparkling glass dessert dishes.

1 baked angel food cake, cubed
2 3-oz. pkgs. strawberry
    gelatin mix
2 c. water

12-oz. pkg. frozen strawberries,
    thawed
8-oz. container frozen whipped
    topping, thawed

Arrange cake cubes in a 2-quart casserole dish; set aside. Combine gelatin mix and water in a bowl, stirring to dissolve. Fold in strawberries and whipped topping; pour over cake. Refrigerate until set. Serves 12.

Before cubing angel food cake, freeze it and then allow it to partially thaw. Fewer crumbs and more cake to enjoy!

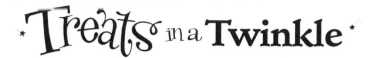

Oatmeal-Raspberry Bars

Elaine Savage
Orland Park, IL

Made in minutes...gone in seconds!

18-1/2 oz. pkg. yellow cake mix
3/4 c. butter, melted
2-1/2 c. quick-cooking oats,
    uncooked

12-oz. jar raspberry jam
1 T. water

Combine dry cake mix, butter and oats in a large bowl; press half of mixture firmly into a greased 13"x9" baking pan. Set aside. Stir jam and water together; spread evenly over cake mixture in pan. Cover with remaining cake mixture; pat firmly over the top. Bake at 375 degrees for 20 minutes; drizzle with Sugar Glaze while warm. Cool; slice into bars to serve. Makes 15 to 18.

Sugar Glaze:

1 c. powdered sugar

2 to 3 T. warm water

Combine powdered sugar with enough water for desired consistency.

Dress up these easy, pleasing bars! Instead of cutting them into bars or squares, cut diagonally across the dish for pretty little diamonds, or use mini cookie cutters for special occasions.

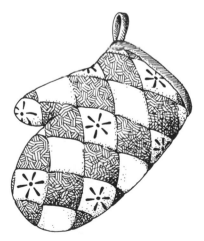

Perfectly Prepared Pantry
Ready-made essentials for speedy suppers!

Breads

biscuit baking mix
flour tortillas
pita bread
quick bread & muffin mixes
refrigerated biscuits
refrigerated bread sticks
refrigerated crescent rolls
refrigerated pizza dough
round buttery crackers
seasoned bread crumbs

Breakfast

flavored yogurt
frozen bagels
frozen waffles & pancakes
precooked bacon
quick-cooking oats
refrigerated cinnamon rolls
granola

Desserts

cake & brownie mixes
chocolate & peanut butter
   chips
frozen whipped topping
fruit preserves
graham cracker pie crusts
ice cream
instant pudding & gelatin
   mixes
maraschino cherries
mini marshmallows
pie fillings
ready-made frosting
refrigerated cookie dough
refrigerated pie crusts

Flavor Boosters

artichoke hearts in a jar
chicken & beef bouillon
dry soup mixes
dry gravy mixes
grated Parmesan cheese
Italian salad dressing
lemon juice
roasted garlic in a jar
roasted red peppers in a jar
salad dressing mixes
shredded cheeses

Perfectly Prepared Pantry
Ready-made essentials for speedy suppers!

Fruits & Veggies

baby carrots
canned beans
canned fruits
canned vegetables
diced, seasoned tomatoes
dried fruit
frozen diced onions &
    peppers
frozen fruits
frozen juice concentrates
canned green chiles
precut celery sticks
raisins

Meat

canned tuna & chicken
cooked, frozen chicken
    breasts
cooked, frozen shrimp
deli sliced ham & turkey

Pasta

frozen ravioli & tortellini
no-boil lasagna noodles
assorted dry pasta

Sauces & Soups

barbecue sauce
canned chicken & beef broth
canned cream soups
canned sloppy joe sauce
gravy in a jar
salsa & picante sauce
tomato paste
tomato sauce
spaghetti & pizza sauce

Sides

frozen veggie blends
seasoned long-grain rice
    blends
refrigerated mashed
    potatoes
bagged salad mix
instant stuffing mix
seasoned pasta mixes

Snacks

microwave popcorn
tortilla chips
pretzels
trail mix
mixed nuts

Market Math

Translate recipes into shopping lists in a flash!

Ingredient:	You need:	Buy:
Apples	1 cup sliced or chopped 1 pound	1 medium 3 medium
Bacon	1/2 cup crisply cooked and crumbled	8 slices
Banana	1 cup mashed	3 medium
Bell Peppers	1/2 cup chopped 1 cup chopped 1-1/2 cups chopped	1 small 1 medium 1 large
Bread Crumbs	1 cup dry 1 cup soft	5 slices toasted 1-1/2 slices
Bread Cubes	1 cup	2 slices
Broccoli	2 cups chopped	1 bunch
Butter	1/2 cup 2 cups	1 stick 1 pound
Carrots	1 cup shredded 2-1/2 cups sliced	1 large 1 pound
Celery	1 cup sliced or chopped	2 medium stalks
Cheese	2 cups shredded	8 ounces
Chocolate	1 cup chips 1 square baking	6 ounces 1 ounce
Corn	1 cup kernels	2 medium ears
Cottage Cheese	2 cups	16 ounces

Market Math

Translate recipes into shopping lists in a flash!

Ingredient:	You need:	Buy:
Cream Cheese	1 cup	8 ounces
Eggs	1 cup beaten 1 cup whites	4 large 6 to 8 large
Flour	3-1/2 cups	1 pound
Garlic	1/2 teaspoon minced	1 medium clove
Graham Crackers	1-1/2 cups crushed	21 squares
Green Beans	4 cups cooked	1 pound fresh
Lemons or Limes	1-1/2 teaspoon zest or 2 to 3 tablespoons juice	1 medium
Lettuce	2 cups shredded 6 cups torn pieces	5 ounces 1 pound
Meat—Beef, Chicken or Pork	1 cup chopped or crumbled	6 ounces
Mushrooms	2-1/2 cups chopped 2/3 cup sliced	8 ounces fresh 4-ounce can
Nuts	1 cup chopped 3 to 4 cups halved	4 ounces, shelled 1 pound
Onions—Green or White	1 tablespoon chopped green 1 cup chopped white	1 medium green 1 large white
Oranges	1 to 2 tablespoons zest 1 cup juice	1 medium 3 medium
Peaches	4 cups sliced	8 medium

Market Math
Translate recipes into shopping lists in a flash!

Ingredient:	You need:	Buy:
Potatoes—White, Red or Sweet	1 cup bite-size cubes or 1 cup sliced	1 medium
Pasta	4 cups cooked macaroni 4 cups cooked egg noodles 4 cups cooked spaghetti	2 cups uncooked 5 cups uncooked 8 ounces uncooked
Rice—Instant, Brown, White or Wild	2 cups cooked instant 4 cups cooked brown 4 cups cooked white 3 cups cooked wild	1 cup uncooked 1 cup uncooked 1 cup uncooked 1 cup uncooked
Saltines	1 cup crushed	29 crackers
Sour Cream	1 cup	8 ounces
Strawberries	2 cups sliced	1 pint fresh
Sugar—Brown, White or Powdered	2-1/4 cups brown, packed 2-1/4 cups white 4 cups powdered	1 pound 1 pound 1 pound
Tomatoes	1/2 cup chopped 1 cup chopped	1 small 1 large
Vanilla Wafers	1-1/2 cups crushed	38 cookies
Whipping Cream	1 cup unwhipped or 2 cups whipped	1/2 pint

Index

Index

Index

Veggies & Salads

Desserts

Find Gooseberry Patch wherever you are!
www.gooseberrypatch.com

Email

Call us toll-free at 1·800·854·6673

U.S. to Metric Recipe Equivalents

Volume Measurements

1/4 teaspoon	1 mL
1/2 teaspoon	2 mL
1 teaspoon	5 mL
1 tablespoon = 3 teaspoons	15 mL
2 tablespoons = 1 fluid ounce	30 mL
1/4 cup	60 mL
1/3 cup	75 mL
1/2 cup = 4 fluid ounces	125 mL
1 cup = 8 fluid ounces	250 mL
2 cups = 1 pint =16 fluid ounces	500 mL
4 cups = 1 quart	1 L

Weights

1 ounce	30 g
4 ounces	120 g
8 ounces	225 g
16 ounces = 1 pound	450 g

Oven Temperatures

300° F	150° C
325° F	160° C
350° F	180° C
375° F	190° C
400° F	200° C
450° F	230° C

Baking Pan Sizes

Square		Loaf	
8x8x2 inches	2 L = 20x20x5 cm	9x5x3 inches	2 L = 23x13x7 cm
9x9x2 inches	2.5 L = 23x23x5 cm	*Round*	
Rectangular		8x1-1/2 inches	1.2 L = 20x4 cm
13x9x2 inches	3.5 L = 33x23x5 cm	9x1-1/2 inches	1.5 L = 23x4 cm

YOUR recipe could appear in our next cookbook!

Share your tried & true family favorites with us instantly at

www.gooseberrypatch.com

If you'd rather jot 'em down by hand, just mail this form to...

Gooseberry Patch • Attn: Cookbook Dept.
PO Box 812 • Columbus, OH 43216-0812

If your recipe is selected for a book, you'll receive a FREE copy!

Please share only your original recipes or those that you have made your own over the years.

Recipe Name:

Number of Servings:

Any fond memories about this recipe? Special touches you like to add
or handy shortcuts?

Ingredients (include specific measurements):

Instructions (continue on back if needed):

Special Code: **cookbookspage**

Over ➤

Extra space for recipe if needed:

Tell us about yourself...

Your complete contact information is needed so that we can send you your FREE cookbook, if your recipe is published. Phone numbers and email addresses are kept private and will only be used if we have questions about your recipe.

Name:

Address:

City: State: Zip:

Email:

Daytime Phone:

Thank you! Vickie & Jo Ann